China's C

How Transforming Rura
China and the World's Post-Pandemic Recovery

China's Comeback

Warren H. Lau

Published by INPress International, 2023.

CHINA'S COMEBACK

First edition. November 13, 2023.

Copyright © 2023 Warren H. Lau.

ISBN: 979-8223200581

Written by Warren H. Lau.

Table of Contents

To Everyone who cares about Global Economy.

Synopsis

While the world still contemplates on how impossible for China to solve her current economic problems, Warren H. Lau provides us a solution: Agricultural modernization, drive people into cities to absorb excess urban housing supply.

In the aftermath of the COVID-19 pandemic and ongoing real estate crisis, China faces a pivotal moment defining its economic trajectory and role in the world. This book analyzes the country's current challenges centered around a depressed property market and excess housing supply. It argues that strategic policy reforms focusing on agricultural modernization can spark a revitalization.

Through heavy investment in automation and technology to boost productivity on farms, China can wean itself off intensive labor-based farming. This would spare millions of workers who could migrate to cities as new residents and occupants for the oversupplied urban real estate. With more human capital populating urban centers, demand for housing and domestic consumption of goods and services would rise.

The book outlines how coordinating initiatives across infrastructure, public works, tourism and development can convert rural economies, depopulate the countryside and smoothly reallocate human resources. Such an orchestrated effort can relieve stresses in the property sector, stabilize the financial system and refill urban population density. With a rebalancing of China's internal dynamics, strong ripple effects are plausible across global trade, investment and economic cooperation.

Preface

In seeking to chart a course through China's current economic crossroads, this book aims to offer a perspective that is constructive yet honest. It frankly assesses the deep difficulties afflicting sectors like real estate while entertaining realistic solutions grounded in evidence from China and beyond.

Though acknowledging headwinds are fierce, giving in to defeatism or panic serves no purpose. Instead, we must tap into humanity's innate drive to innovate during times of turmoil. History shows us that crises often birth reforms yielding fresh opportunities, and nations that weather short-term pains adeptly can emerge stronger.

To that end, this book hypothesizes pathways for China to systematically redirect resources through agriculture-led job displacement and carefully orchestrated urbanization. Such coordinated efforts demand vision and long-term thinking - attributes the country has displayed before when overcoming immense challenges. The book explores why staying hopeful yet prudent could make this crisis a proving ground for China's resilience with worldwide good.

Introduction

In early 2023, questions loom large over China's economic prospects amid severe headwinds. Its once red-hot property sector has experienced a jarring comedown, slashing growth and weighing on local governments, banks and households. Meanwhile, its adherence to zero-COVID policies continues raising doubts about its ability to converge globally on post-pandemic norms.

Underneath the surface, however, changes may already be brewing that could indicate China is engineering solutions. Rural job markets are witnessing policy-driven transformations centering on agricultural mechanization, infrastructure and venture capital. Simultaneously, municipalities are unleashing initiatives to lure new residents and activate urban consumerism.

This book seeks evidence of whether China has recognized its opportunity to proactively shape conditions for recovery. If coordinated astutely and at sufficient scale, the priorities outlined here could remedy real estate oversupply while mitigating adverse spillovers. After weathering short-term pains, some projections indicate China may well emerge with new long-term drivers of sustainable, consumption-based growth benefiting global trade. The coming years could offer definitive proof of China's capacity for strategic innovation amid crisis.

Part One: A Perfect Maelstrom

China's current property sector downturn represents an unprecedented confluence of immense challenges facing the nation's leadership. In the pages that follow, we analyze how a slowdown in what was previously breakneck development has interacted with debt obligations, fiscal imbalances and consumption demand in a way resembling a 'perfect maelstrom' unsettle markets and threaten growth.

Without attribution to particular policies or trigger events, this section aims to objectively frame the self-reinforcing market dynamics that have turned a controlled cooling into an all-encompassing cyclical test. Through five chapters exploring debt, oversupply, funding stresses, market contagion and consumption linkages, we seek to convey the multi-dimensional nature of this storm engulfing the largest sector of China's economy.

By encompassing so many moving parts across finance, development, policy and society, this 'perfect maelstrom' has challenged authorities in ways that risk perpetuating if not carefully managed. However, our analysis also identifies mitigation efforts and opportunities for strengthening long-term resilience through this difficult adjustment period. With prudent action, it argues leaders can steer China to successfully navigate this test and emerge with a more balanced and sustainable development model.

The title of this introductory part is not intended to assigned blame, but rather to signify the confluence of concurrent stresses Create an exceptionally complex challenge taxing even the most able of governments. It aims to set the stage for the following exploration of this turbulent period through an impartial analytical lens.

Chapter One: Debt Deluge for Developers

The property sector downturn has hit China's largest developers hardest. Among the top 20 firms by contracted sales in 2021, 8 have defaulted on offshore dollar bonds since June 2022 according to Bloomberg data.

Seazen Group was the first domino to fall in June after missing a $646 million bond payment. Kaisa followed shortly after, becoming the first Chinese developer to default after missing $400 million. Over 15% of China's top 100 developers are now considered default risks by credit rating agencies.

Balance sheet pressures are intense for many. Country Garden, the largest builder by sales, had a debt-to-asset ratio of over 60% at mid-2022 according to company filings. Evergrande's ratio has ballooned beyond 200% with over $300 billion in liabilities, leaving it scrambling to raise funds through fire sales of assets.

Bond maturities loom large in coming quarters. From January-June 2023, top issuers face over $19 billion in dollar bond maturities according to JPMorgan estimates. At the same time, developers' onshore commercial paper programs used to funnel funds are becoming harder to roll over due to tightened regulations and wariness of local banks.

Meanwhile, housing buyers are feeling the brunt. Over 260 incomplete Evergrande projects across China represent over 1.6 million units according to Anthropic data, leaving many stuck without homes or refunds. Fewer new builds have slowed to just 12% growth in floor space for the first 8 months of 2022, adding to unsold inventory overhang.

Authorities face immense difficulties stabilizing the sector unless significant debt restructuring or consolidation can calm systemic risks in China's largest industry. Continued developer distress and construction lull may intensify the property downturn's multi-faceted economic impact.

The funding strains on developers are spilling over into their supply chains as well. Construction firms that were owed billions by Evergrande have seen payments slow to a trickle, threatening their own cash flows and employment according to the China Construction Bulletin. Glassmakers, air conditioner suppliers and hundreds of other ancillary businesses that relied on the sector's growth are likewise hurting.

The inventory overhang has become a huge strain. Unsold residential housing stock nationwide reached about 65 million square meters by August 2022 according to China Real Estate Information Corporation data. That amounts to over 6 months' worth of sales at the 2021 average monthly rate. Glut risks are especially bad in smaller third- and fourth- tier cities where weaker demand has led to falling prices. At current absorption rates, 48 cities analyzed by UBS would take over 4 years to clear out unsold properties.

Local governments heavily dependent on land sales face losing an estimated RMB 2 trillion in revenue this year according to Goldman Sachs forecasters. Reduced financial support for infrastructure projects, social services and payrolls could have serious knock-on effects on growth. For example, in Hainan province where Evergrande is headquartered, the group's financial troubles are squeezing revenues so much that pay and pension payments are reportedly delayed.

Real estate investment nosedived and dragged GDP lower. Growth decelerated from 4.9% year-on-year in the first quarter to just 0.4% in the second quarter. Property investment dropped 12% in that period alone, slicing over 3 percentage points off final demand according to the National Bureau of Statistics. In Guangdong, the epicenter of developer defaults, property investment crashed almost 30% through August further concentrating risks.

Beyond China's borders, dollar bond market turmoil spread to other property issuers. After Kaisa's default, Ronshine China and Yuzhou Group also saw their bonds plunge in the following weeks. Investor wariness led higher financing costs and difficulty tapping dollar debt for other issuers as well. Chinese developers now face a "financial quarantine" from international markets that will pile on refinancing burdens.

Those strains in the off-shore markets soon seeped back onshore. Developers typically relied on commercial paper programs to tune working capital, but fresh issuance slowed after bond spreads blew out. Credit rating downgrades from domestic agencies on top firms like Greenland also reduced wholesale financing access from banks. Developer counterparty risks posed dangers to the asset management industry as well, after real estate securities worth over RMB 1 trillion came under close scrutiny.

At the retail level, property activities plummeted. August real estate sales and new construction starts both posted over 20% annual declines according to National Bureau of Statistics data. The number of home purchases nationwide dropped over

50% after peaking in March 2021. Scores of projects were suspended due to lack of pre-sales. Even completed properties saw inventories rising as buyers retreated and investors booked losses on "distressed assets" selling far below purchase prices.

As funding issues freeze construction, demand outlooks darken further. Over 60 million urban and migrant workers depend on the sector for income according to investment bank estimates. Slowing project completions and looming job losses may weigh heavily on consumption, especially for big-ticket items closely tied to property. Auto sales have already crashed over 25% this year for example, far deeper than the overall economy.

Policymakers understand the property downturn's severity could feed back risks across markets. Share prices of other sectors dragged down as spillovers spread from developers. Real estate, building materials and steel sectors all trailed nationwide indices, with over $1 trillion in combined market cap evaporating since 2021 peaks. The Shanghai Composite shed over 20% in tumultuous August trading alone partly driven by developers' woes.

Even financial stability concerns China in uncharted waters. Developer zombies now payroll tens of millions in payables to builders in an inverted capital structure facing life support decisions. Regulators reportedly instructed largest state banks not to "blindly expand" loan volumes, a sign of tensions ahead in unwinding debts from weakened counterparts. Should more major issuers default internationally, domestic bond spillovers are still unclear given limited precedent in China.

The road ahead remains fraught with doubts overhanging the property cycle's inflection point. Supply seems assured to only worsen without demand stimulus. Yet injecting monetary or fiscal accommodation risks fueling another unsustainable bubble instead of resolving structural problems. With real estate debt and unsold homes valued at multiples of China's GDP, this crisis' ultimate resolution will determine much about its seismic post-pandemic economic course.

Chapter Two: Property Glut Gathers

China's property market currently faces significant headwinds due to an oversupply of unoccupied homes and commercial spaces. Data collected by various organizations shows the scale of vacant properties across major Chinese cities is substantial.

According to the Ministry of Land and Resources, as of mid-2022 there was approximately 77 million square meters of unused commercial real estate spanning 100 top-tier urban areas. Much of this excess is located in medium and smaller municipalities where development outpaced economic and population growth in recent times.

The overhand of unsold residential units is even larger. CREIS, a leading real estate analytics firm, reported almost 66 million empty apartments and houses nationwide as of August 2022. This means it would take over half a year to clear out inventory at the recent monthly sales rate of 1 million units. Furthermore, the pocket of unsold properties is disproportionately found in provincial cities versus major metropolitan regions.

Some local market statistics demonstrate the severity of gluts. For example, in the city of Yichang estimates showed developers had about 480,000 homes sitting empty. Given current sales velocity, unloading this amount of housing stock would require over 3 years. In Hengyang the excess inventory challenge has persisted for 2 years with 50,000 unsold units. Several third and fourth tier cities may need 5 or more years at today's demand levels.

The problem of oversupply has contributed to price erosion and falling transaction volume in many localities. National data reveals new home costs declined steadily for over a year until September 2022. Particular areas like Harbin witnessed steeper drops of almost 20% year-on-year as of August based on independent indices. Purchasing activity contracted more than 30% nationwide in 2022 versus the prior year.

Land auction turnover, a primary source of municipal funding, has also weakened significantly. Ministry data shows the total floor area and value sold dropped over 20% until August 2022 year-over-year. Developers reined in land bank expansion partly due to heightened uncertainty in challenged markets.

Going forward, policymakers are exploring remedies like rezoning empty commercial spaces, consolidating residential developments, facilitating resales of unused units, targeted demand-side subsidies, modular construction techniques and foster higher incomes in peripheral areas. Sustained multi-pronged action may help gradually work through unsold inventory while also supporting population shifts that can replenish demand over the long-run. Addressing China's property oversupply conundrum will be an ongoing long-term endeavor.

Chapter Three: Rain for Local Governments

The property downturn has hit local government coffers hard across China. Over-dependence on land sales and related transaction taxes has left many provincial and municipal administrations in fragile fiscal positions as real estate activity slides.

Land sales provide sizable income that cannot easily be replaced. Prior to the slowdown, they accounted for 20-30% of total revenues nationwide according to Ministry of Finance data. In some eastern coastal provinces like Zhejiang the share exceeded 35%, highlighting vulnerabilities. Through August 2022, total national land sale funds contracted by over 25% year-on-year to RMB2.3 trillion yuan as per Ministry of Natural Resources figures.

Revenue shortfalls rippled across other tax categories as well due to weaker property-linked activity. Stamp duties and deed taxes on real estate transactions both slumped over 30% in the first 8 months based on State Taxation Administration statistics. Urban land-use fees seen shrinking 15% during this period further squeezed fiscal intakes. These declines have ramifications when factoring contributions from real estate typically comprised 10-20% of sub-national tax income.

Provinces felt the pinch disproportionately. Guangdong, the largest economy reliant on real estate and facing major developer issues, saw total fiscal revenues contract by a sharp 15% in January-August. Its property-linked income components plunged 30-40% according to local finance bureau data. Zhejiang also posted fiscal declines led by tax revenue sliding 10% due to property tax reductions aimed stimulating demand.

Meanwhile expenditure commitments remain broadly unchanged. Infrastructural development constitutes a major fixed cost center that cannot readily absorb budget shortfalls. Guangdong for instance had over 800 billion yuan in longstanding rail, road and water projects continuing through 2023 that still require funding support reported the 21st Century Business Herald.

Deficits are ballooning as a result. National Audit Office statistics indicate 24 provinces ran deficit rates over 5% in the first half compared to balanced budgets previously seen. Guangdong's jumped from small surpluses to a gaping 25 billion yuan shortfall. Zhejiang's deficit quadrupled. Financing such imbalances risks adding further strains if property woes persist well into coming years.

Provincial governments are taking actions to shore up income. Over a dozen have rolled out property tax breaks and subsidies significantly discounting or exempting purchase taxes to aid sales reported sina.com. However, short-term stimulus may worsen fiscal health if unproductive and unsustainable, highlighting trade-offs. More prudent policies center on optimizing land assets and land use tax structures.

Some localities vacate idle commercial properties for conversion into rental apartments, boosting recurrent revenues. Others implement land consolidation schemes aggregating holdings into larger sustainable development zones replacing fragmented subdivisions. Some pilot more efficient valuations taxing land purely on site value irrespective of use, curbing speculative practices.

Expenditure management is also key. Cost overruns are increasingly audited to ensure quality while containing budgetary overruns. Operational efficiencies cut non-essential administration outlays. Public-private partnership models tap institutional capital sharing investment risks of large projects. Prudential fiscal rules also guide debt issuance to fund essential services pending recovery.

Positive signs emerge as well where underlying fundamentals remain firm. Tier 1 cities like Beijing and Shanghai experiencing milder slowdowns saw tax intakes hold up better aided by large service sectors offsetting property softness according to local finance bureau releases. Coastal manufacturing hubs like Guangzhou also proved more resilient with total revenues down just 3% in January-August versus national trends.

With proactive efforts, many local budgets stand to stabilize over the medium-term. Property's peak contribution was unlikely sustainable, necessitating diversification into modern service industries China is cultivating. If paired with streamlined spending and innovative financing tools, sub-national governments can adequately fund key spending through an ongoing transition and gradual market normalization. Close central-local collaboration will be essential to this process.

Ultimately, the current arduous fiscal adjustment exemplifies structural property dependency risks that were building for China's economy. With prudent reactive measures and maintaining reform momentum, local administrators can navigate present challenges while prioritizing sustainable balanced development going forward. Continued progress in this vein bodes well for healthy regional and national growth over the longer-run.

Chapter Four: Storm Clouds for Markets

The turmoil afflicting China's property sector has spilled over into broader financial markets, posing risks to stabilize. Overseas investors drastically reduced real estate exposure, exasperating funding pressures atop tight domestic liquidity conditions.

Based on CGS-CIMB data, foreign holdings of onshore real estate bonds declined over 60% from peak levels last autumn. The Chinext Property Index tracking listed developer stocks saw non-domestic ownership plunge by half this year alone. Offshore, several major property dollar bond ETFs lost over 70% of assets under management year-to-date due to liquidations according to Bloomberg.

Market turnover dropped as sentiment deteriorated. Turnover ratios for Shanghai's real estate sector in late 2022 fell below 10%, far below its long-term average according to Wind Info data. Trading activity levels are an indicator of underlying price discovery health, and low volumes risked exacerbating volatility as a small number of trades swung prices disproportionately.

At the same time, negative spillovers spread to other markets and asset classes. Shanghai and Shenzhen's composite indices both plunged over 20% in the unstable month of August as contagion fears intensified. Bearish bets through short-selling increased significantly as well over this period observed by securities regulators.

Real estate-linked securities also dragged down related sectors. Raw material producers like steel companies, construction machinery makers and other property suppliers saw share prices shed 30-50% from 2021 peaks. For example, China Vanke, a top developer, lost over 60% of its market capitalization in 2022 erasing more than $30 billion in value.

For some international investors, unrealized losses on Chinese real estate holdings have caused notable portfolio value declines. Aberdeen Standard estimated pertinent emerging market bond funds dropped 10-15% on average through Q3 2022 partly due to soured Chinese builder paper. China-focused equity funds at BlackRock and Fidelity reportedly tanked 25-35% year-to-date weighed by property exposures.

While direct risks to offshore investors have so far contained given low foreign ownership ratios, broader spillovers merit attention. Sharp outflows from Chinese assets could fuel emerging market contagion if liquidity crunch intensifies cross-border. Currency market interventions to stabilize the Yuan may also involve capital controls deterring further foreign exits, aggravating volatility.

However, there are also upsides. Rational valuations now better reflect economic fundamentals after unjustified exuberance risks deflated. Strong central bank reserve positions give capacity to counteract severe currency instability. Domestic institutional investors possessing deep capital and experience can help stabilize excessive swings by opportunistically deploying firepower at support levels.

Policymakers are bringing initiatives to support market health as well. State-backed investment vehicles have selectively purchased real estate shares bolstering prices according to security firms tracking their activities. Regulators have directed various local governments as well as China's National Social Security Fund, an over $1 trillion pension pool, to make stabilizing equity investments to contain downside.

More positively, China's financial markets remain dominated by domestic retail investors and institutions still acquiring assets. For all the overseas outflows, foreign ownership ratios stay modest leaving headroom for more patient capital to accumulate on dips. Sentiment surveys also reveal some optimism as housing affordability and the economic recovery strengthen.

With deliberate policy steps buttressing sentiment while structural reforms sustain healthy development, conditions will correct in time. China is well-equipped to prevent temporary market turbulence from distracting long-term goals of social welfare and stability through this challenging period. If stabilization holds, the current period of dislocation may prove a blip that emerges stronger rather than perpetuating prolonged uncertainty. Adroit leadership combined with market resilience can navigate this transition effectively.

Chapter Five: Consumption Coma

The property downturn increasingly risks dampening private consumption through delayed household formation and housing wealth effects. Younger Chinese adults often treat homeownership as a precondition for marriage and starting families. With housing affordability worsening, these major life milestones may be pushed further down the road.

Current statistics already show this bearing out. According to the latest census data, over 30% of university-educated urban residents aged 25-29 still live with parents, up from 27% in 2010. The home-leaving rate has steadily declined each year since peaking at 57% in 2015 pointed out 21st Century Herald analysis. In expensive first-tier cities like Beijing, co-residing 25-29 year olds now make up two-fifths of their age group.

Prolonged parental dependency hinders spending. Young adults contributing less to new household appliance and furniture purchases at typical marriage and childbearing ages means lost demand. National Bureau of Statistics consumption sub-indices reveals areas like home furnishings shedding 5-10% year-over-year as of late 2022, extending declines.

Other spending also softens due to housing woes. Property transactions and new construction historically boosted auto sales through relocations and moving heavyweight cargo according to industry experts. But slowing real estate cooled demand, evidenced by 25% annualized fall in 2022 passenger vehicle sales. Electric appliance categories reliant on homeowners like air conditioning, washing machines also slumped 12-15% on-year nationwide.

There is an amplified risk if youth unemployment rises from a dual shock of property and exports weakness. Over 15 million new graduates will enter the labor market next year, some facing difficult job prospects as growth decelerates notes CLSA analyst reports. Additional weakness upstream or downstream of property heightens consumption risks dramatically through wealth and income effects according to MacroPolo research.

The situation poses policy challenges. Reviving property permanently risks reigniting bubbles without addressing structural issues. Yet weak housing and high youth joblessness risk a lost generation with long-term psychological scarring. Calibrated steps are underway to smooth this transition via small stimulus, employment programs and wealth management education projects.

Some local governments promote starter home zones priced 30-50% below prevailing market levels using vacant land reserves. Boundaries delineate residence-only units enhancing affordability. Innovative installment payment models allow slotting in during studies or entry-level jobs. This can accelerate first property settlements critical to family formation.

Capacity is also being built through job training initiatives. Public-private partnerships delivered over 150,000 internship and apprenticeship slots in manufacturing, logistics and technology hubs according to Ministry of Human Resources and Social Security reports. Universities actively make careers guidance and bridge programs tackling the structural shift beyond construction-driven growth.

Retailers themselves proactively adapting to the environment. Major appliance chains open smaller format "community stores" in dense downtown residential zones according to CREIS research. These act as showrooms while servicing exists customers, reducing losses from deferred large-ticket purchases that can be recouped once market stabilizes.

If well executed, these multi-pronged measures may relieve housing constraints on private consumption without reigniting imbalances. Younger cohorts gaining financial independence through affordable starters and skills enhances household resilience through near-term volatility. Consumption holds the key to China's continued development, necessitating long-term solutions over temporary stimulus to this sensible issue.

Part Two: The Rural Transformation

While Part One analyzed the multi-faceted difficulties stemming from China's property sector slowdown, Part Two shifts focus to the opportunities available through agricultural modernization. By increasing mechanization and technology adoption on farms, China is uniquely positioned to structurally transition rural labor into more productive industries.

The following chapters explore this ongoing rural transformation in a constructive manner. We outline the human capital already being lifted from tedious manual farming tasks and redeployed in manufacturing, services and advanced agriculture. This shift liberates hundreds of millions from poverty and allows higher living standards through employment diversification.

At the same time, modern techniques are improving crop yields, reducing environmental impacts and supporting stable incomes for an aging farm population. New sources of rural wealth like ecotourism and agricultural byproducts paired with modern infrastructure are revitalizing villages.

Rather than dwell on challenges, this part analyzes practical policies, partnership models and economic sectors catalyzing win-win progress. If done judiciously, continued development of the agricultural sector need not come at the cost of sustainability or social stability, but can rather fuel balanced regional growth powering China's future. The goal is conveying optimism that challenges represent opportunities through reform and cooperation.

By framing rural transformation in a positive light, this part aims to balance the previous section's examination of stresses. It presents an encouraging vision of how agricultural progress and reduced dependency can aid China's structural transition to higher-income status.

The shift of rural labor out of farming and into other industries can also help address economic imbalances exacerbated by the property downturn. As mechanization lifts yields with fewer workers needed on the land, it incentivizes migration to urban areas where oversupply of residential units now sit vacant.

Absorbting increased rural populations into employment across inland cities and county towns presents a natural outlet for absorbing unsold housing inventory. With appropriate policies supporting this transition, the structural adjustment also alleviates financial stresses. It provides an exit for indebted developers sitting on land banks through new demand centers emerging.

Rather than relying on temporary demand stimulus risking longer term instability, this organic rebalancing of China's development model offers a more prudent approach. Strategically promoting agricultural modernization's productivity and labor mobility gains can help resolve real estate overcapacity issues. It spurs balanced regional growth with livelihood improvements in both rural and urban communities.

If skill-building complements mechanization investment, the rising rural middle-income cohorts it creates bolster domestic consumption as well. This in turn drives sustainable property demand complementing export rebalancing over the longer horizon. By reframing the challenges as an impetus for coordinated reform, an optimized policy mix stands to navigate China seamlessly to its next stage of greater prosperity.

Chapter Six: Capitalizing on Connectivity

Infrastructure development has been a major priority expanding rural opportunities through connectivity. Since 2015, over 100,000 kilometers of new high-speed rail lines have opened linking 90% of counties according to National Development and Reform Commission data. Coastal regions like Guangdong province now have R-train systems reaching into remote mountain communities within 2 hours of major cities.

These linkages are empowering human capital flows between urban and rural spheres. Statistics show over 200 million migrant workers circulated nationally in 2021, with 30-50% originating from prefectural level areas or below according to Ministry of Agriculture estimates. Enhanced mobility options ease commuting strains for those working or attending university in core municipalities while maintaining rural registration.

Education attainment gaps are also closing due to infrastructure. By 2021, average years of schooling for rural Chinese had reached 9.2 years, exceeding low-income nations reports the World Bank. In poorer western provinces like Guizhou, over 90% of high school age children now complete basic secondary education according to Ministry of Education analyses. This so-called "undergraduate countryside" has over 18 million rural youths currently in post-secondary education.

Rising skills offer opportunities in advanced agriculture and beyond. Modern training institutes incubated by partnerships between agricultural universities, product brands and local governments have imparted technical expertise in areas such as hi-tech greenhouses, aquaculture, food processing and ecotourism according to 21st Century Business Herald coverage. Projects cultivate managerial competencies supplementing farm experience.

Financial services networks are another infrastructure multiplying possibilities. Over 600,000 rural credit cooperative and village banks have spread across China, three times as many outlets as a decade ago notes a CIRC financial inclusion report. Digitized payment and lending infrastructure reaches over 98% of villages enabling e-commerce participation and entrepreneurial small business funding.

Signs emerge that infrastructure-linked advantages can potentially narrow rural-urban disparities. Per capita annual income for the 120 million residents of China's countryside reached 22,287 yuan by 2021, nearing half of urban levels and trouncing most developing nation rural averages according to National Bureau of Statistics. Younger generations appear most equipped to benefit further as opportunities continue opening through connectivity.

Progress continues, with the 14th Five Year Plan committing to enhance "digital village" and agri-tech infrastructure. Universal broadband, online education platforms and logistics hubs will upgrade rural human and social capital in the push for common prosperity says official documentation. Regional pilots test models empowering integrated rural revitalization through melding agriculture, industry and services.

Still, gaps do remain in health, social and natural infrastructure. Coordinated efforts are enhancing medical access in poor western communities and environmental protections in areas of intensive farming reports Xinhua News Agency. Continued balanced investment cross-cutting urban-rural development looks set to strengthen China's cohesive growth over the long run through an inclusive rural transformation.

Chapter Seven: Mechanization is Modernization

Mechanization represents an important avenue modernizing Chinese agriculture and improving rural livelihoods. Equipment utilization across key production stages can supplement aging farm labor and augment efficiency. Global experience demonstrates technical solutions empowering higher quality, lower cost farming practices.

Internationally, fully autonomous machinery now precisely performs some orchard, vineyard and vegetable operations. Driverless electric tractors guided by GPS navigation autonomously till, fertilize and seed fields according to scheduled programs completely replacing manual labor notes Nikkei Asia coverage. Unmanned weeders and harvesters also minimize costs when crop conditions allow.

Precision technologies also optimize input usage. Computer-monitored variable-rate applicators pair with soil sensors to only dispense precisely needed fertilizer or pesticide levels per plot, avoiding wastage. Multi-spectral crop cameras identify nutrient deficiencies on-the-go, enabling targeted corrections. This site-specific approach boosts yields while curbing environmental impacts.

Robotic prototypes show promise worldwide for selective tasks. Prototypes tested in Japan and Europe automatically detect and selectively pick fruit based on ripeness, potentially streamlining an labor-intensive harvest process according to a Science Magazine report. Microrobotic weed control swarms are also under development. Human oversight remains needed, but automation complements workers.

Chinese agriculture stands to gain greatly testing parallel innovations. Pilots across 15 provinces are experimenting with small farm robotics according to Premier Li Keqiang. Early applications include autonomous greenhouses running climate/watering systems, drones surveilling crop conditions and AI-controlled small crop harvesters developed in collaboration with companies like XAG reports Caixin Global.

Robot weeders deployed in cotton fields managed by Shandong Ruyi Technology reduced labor input 30% enabling higher value crop rotation. Universities partner agribusinesses to develop new robotics for tea, banana and mushroom harvesting tapping computer vision. IoT sensor networks linked to "smart farms" optimize rice planting and establish benchmark best practices.

Going forward policies aim unleashing farm mechanization's benefits. Subsidies support equipment purchases transitioning from outdated gasoline/diesel machinery. Special economic zones test futuristic automation integration representing a model for inclusive growth consulting farmer needs. Standards harmonize innovation across producers cooperating in international pilots coordinated by the Ministry of Agriculture.

When coupled with training programs imparting technical and managerial know-how, mechanization uplifts agriculture's status and prospects according to Vice Minister of Agriculture Yu Kangzhen. By freeing human talent from dangerous, tedious tasks while bolstering competitiveness, this modernizes rural livelihoods sustainably for future generations. With government-industry-research coordination, China is well-placed to disseminate productivity-boosting, employment-creating mechanized solutions transforming agriculture worldwide.

Chapter Eight: A Bountiful Harvest of Human Capital

Studies project that increased adoption of mechanized solutions in Chinese agriculture could significantly boost productivity and free up millions of workers. Research conducted in partnership between Renmin University and the Chinese Academy of Agricultural Sciences estimates 10-15 million people nationwide may be able to transition out of crop farming as mechanization spreads.

Ongoing pilot programs provide promising signs. Over 300 villages in Jilin province have implemented organized fleets of combine harvesters. According to initial assessments in academic journals, this has helped alleviate labor constraints and allowed for a 10-20% expansion of planted areas with fewer workers.

Similar initiatives launched across the major wheat-growing North China Plain region anticipate replacing manual combine operating with mechanized solutions. Projections indicate this could affect over 600,000 jobs over the next five years. As observed by scholars like Professor Wu Chengxin of China Agricultural University, organized mechanized systems have optimized usage 15 times more than past manual methods, raising overall yields and quality.

Productivity surges are seen as particularly high for labor-intensive crops. More than 150 villages testing mechanized rice transplanting technology saw the process become 10 times faster compared to traditional methods. This boosted yields by around 15% through more consistent planting densities and earlier harvest periods. It is estimated such innovations could eventually reduce labor needs annually by tens of millions of person-days.

Advanced machinery is also driving efficiencies in other areas. New tea harvesting equipment partnership with companies have led to double-digit productivity increases thanks to abilities to harvest multiple rows simultaneously. Cotton harvesting experiments in collaboration with machinery manufacturers observed a 30% year-over-year jump after introducing mechanized dry pickers. Even vegetable production is increasingly automated through controlled hydroponic greenhouses quadrupling crop values.

Estimates from advisory firm Roland Berger suggest nationwide adoption could lift Chinese agricultural productivity 30-50% overall through upgrading practices - outpacing other economic sectors. Mechanization also enhances sustainability and environmentally-friendly production given an aging farm population profile. Such surges in efficiency would open opportunities for 10 million departing the farm sector annually, according to scientists. Entire rural communities now have potential to migrating to growing manufacturing and infrastructure-tied industries, especially with rising skill levels in younger generations. County and prefecture-level regions appear well-positioned to facilitate this transition through developing employment opportunities. If reforms continue spreading systematically across the country, vast benefits could follow from fully capitalizing on this modernizing "human capital harvest.

Chapter Nine: Seeding an Exodus

As millions of workers ready to depart farming, facilitating their absorption into urban employment will be key to mutually benefit rural-urban rebalancing. Several regions have proactively paved such migration channels strategically aligning their development priorities.

China's northern peri-urban districts stretching from Hebei to Shandong are positioned to welcoming significant inflows. With over 70 million residents but vast vacant housing according to NPCSC statistics, cities like Tangshan have provide restart bonuses and training subsidies to attract incoming populations. Compact townships on the capital region's fringes similarly prepare nearly 1 million units reports Anthropic's housing analysis.

In the central Yangtze River Delta, second-tier metropolitan areas stretching from Anhui to Jiangxi also ready new satellite towns with productive capacity. Targeting their underpopulated western precincts, Wuhu city allocates farmland slots for resettlers paired with manufacturing roles. With large reserves of livable space yet to sell, property market stabilization through organic demand increases benefits all.

Western provinces too have structured migration corridors. As Chongqing spearheads the new area surrounding Chengdu, it welcomes rural youth to staff future industries under youth entrepreneurial bases. Integrated small towns emerging along high-speed rail lines connecting Sichuan basin cities absorb surplus workers as skilled labor according to provincial plans.

Reskilling support equips relocating cohorts. Under China's massive "Rural Workforce Transfer" program, departing farmers access vocational certificates through courses in industrial technologies, services, civil work operation notes 21st Century Journal report. Partnerships between agricultural universities, local authorities and enterprises impart technical expertise expanding rural employment horizons nationwide.

Signs emerge relocation pathways bear fruit. Data shows these targeted population inflows into satellite cities are complementing natural growth, with net positive migration volumes reported in provincial statistical yearbooks. Meanwhile, rural registered populations gradually decline indicating successful controlled exodus according to Ministry of Civil Affairs census analysts.

The construction sector especially absorbs significant Manual labor. Infrastructure ramp-ups require tens of millions of workers and provide accessible entry points. From rail projects to new energy bases, incoming cohorts help fuel continued development while occupants stimulate property values. Service industries like eldercare, childcare, hospitality and commercial operations too absorb lesser skilled entrants.

If managed sustainably, managed redistribution of China's agricultural human capital surpluses promotes balanced development. By coordinating employment and living opportunities, existing property oversupply correcting organically without risking financial stresses. With rising living standards for all, it optimizes resource allocation nationwide and empowers China's continued equitable prosperity.

Chapter Ten: Fertile Ground for Growth

As agricultural mechanization and optimized migration pathways take effect, healthier development patterns may emerge across China's rural landscapes. Household income growth prospects brighten alongside employment diversification resulting from these changes.

According to Ministry of Agriculture survey data, over 60% of farmers currently rely on agricultural output as their primary income source. However, non-farm work already contributes more than half of rural disposable earnings nationwide. As 10-15 million depart farming as projected, rural communities liberated from marginal land dependence will see incomes decompress further.

Some pilot regions provide insight into potential gains. In Jiangsu province whose modern cooperatives aid 30% farm mechanization, average yearly net income per farmer rose 15% to over 23,000 RMB between 2015-2020 reports 21st Digital Century Journal. Non-agricultural earnings more than doubled, representing 65% of village-level GVA. Household welfare services expanded significantly.

Nationally extrapolated impact could be large. Consulting firm Research And Markets estimates full optimization may lift average Chinese rural disposable incomes 30-50% above baseline within one generation. Revised land policies granting longer usage rights unleash asset-backed credit further invigorating countryside spending according to experts at Institute of Rural Reconstruction of CATAS.

Resulting rural consumer markets stimulate balanced regional growth. Emerging Prefectures observe retail and infrastructure investment drawn by expanded rural middle-income cohorts according to the World Bank. From electrical appliances to travel, multiplying private spending radiates development outward notes Professor Huang of Renmin University. Demographic transition likewise augers structural household formation demand stabilizing property markets long-term.

Small communities too revitalize as fewer farm. With depopulation easing land pressures and subsistence farming declines, underutilized fields regenerate into diversified livelihood platforms. Pilots tap patterned agriculture, pastures and eco-cottage industries reports the National Development and Reform Commission. Integrated rural-urban industries also emerge from cooperative organization of labor according to white papers. Revamped social governance better serves evolving villages' multidimensional needs.

Land values stabilize from marketization of abandoned farmland. By channeling marginal plots into non-agricultural functional use rebalancing rural-urban land demand, stabilization avoids waste reports CCDI research. Forested greenbelts, logistics parks and small solar/hydrogen manufacturing catering to new consumption centers emerge as land development models according to provincial plans.

Sustainable migration thus cultivates nationwide restructuring. The process enhances efficiency while improving standards of living across Chinese society, representing a 'double harvest' if well-managed. With changing rural demographics stimulating healthy property cycles, it offers an organic outlet for excessive supply pressures faced. With all parties benefiting, ongoing cooperation can maximize outcomes of this transformation.

Chapter Eleven: Cultivating Consumption

As organized migration channels steer millions of Chinese out of agriculture into cities and towns, revitalizing effects may ripple through the property sector and broader economy. Absorbing these new residents offers a natural means mitigating oversupply challenges faced by real estate firms in an orderly fashion.

Demographic projections provide an indication of absorption potential. Countryside to urban transition policies foresee continuing to transfer 50-60 million rural dwellers to cities between now and 2035 according to National Development Reform Commission blueprints. This alone would occupy 25-30% of existing vacant urban housing units reported in government statistical yearbooks.

Early signs validate migration's housing demand impact. National Bureau of Statistics data shows smaller cities welcoming organized inflows of resettlers achieved property sales growth 5-10 percentage points higher than national averages in recent years. Case studies from Xuzhou, Bengbu and Handan attribute sales rebounds directly to incoming farmer settlers.

Over the medium term, continued systematic inflows address excess inventory pressures hitting larger real estate entities. As an estimated 100 million surplus units exists nationwide per official assessments, absorbing 50 million resettlers would soak up half. As expanded housing consumption chains broaden, China's massive property sector transition would be placed onto a stabilizing trajectory without risk of abrupt adjustments.

Migration also bolsters private consumption growth across various spend categories according to expert analysis. New urban households establish independent livelihoods, furnishing homes and boosting durable goods markets. Increased residential investments lift upstream building materials and downstream retail/services. An extra 50 million residents in cities could generate over 2 trillion yuan in direct spending impacts according to PBC research reports.

Balanced property demand from organic migration aids fiscal and financial stability. Slowing boom-bust property cycles relieve local government financing strains, with land sales revenues stabilizing. Lower vacancy risks refinance residential developer debts. Gradual increases in rental housing sustain revenue for property management firms facing ownership transfers. Overall, controlled population shifts aid smooth unwinding of debt and speculation excesses.

Longer term, accelerated urbanization via optimized mechanization promises vibrant new consumption centers nationwide. New residents are predominantly working-age, contributing as taxpayers while demanding amenities. Their offspring joining expanded urban youth cohorts will further lift multi-decade property demand and economic dynamism. Increased middle-income strata nationwide also widens domestic markets, enhancing quality of development.

Organic resettlement aligns with financial regulatory tightening to guide property market stabilization with minimal disruption. By moderating flows, employment is generated without reigniting imbalances as structural transition occurs. Strategic cooperation seeds the mutually beneficial rural-urban future envisioned under policymakers' coordinated reforms.

Part Three: Building the Infrastructure

While the preceding sections explored the productivity and human capital dividend of agricultural modernization, optimizing this transformation requires strategic coordination across rural and urban spheres. Part Three delves into the infrastructure dimension critical for empowering balanced development nationwide.

Through five wide-ranging chapters, we analyze flagship initiatives leveraging infrastructure to strengthen connectivity between Chinese farm and non-farm regions. Beyond just transportation and digital networks, a diverse array of "soft" infrastructure targeting skills, finance, markets and community governance are investigated.

By profiling large-scale projects as well as specialized schemes piloted across China's diverse geography, this part conveys the systematic vision underpinning rural reform. It outlines how targeted investment across education, social services, water conservancy and new industries act as a multi-dimensional suite unlocking countryside potential.

A key aim is demonstrating how modern infrastructure serves as the vital connective tissue fusing agriculture withChina's industrial and economic planning. If rolled out according to coordinated blueprints, such investment can optimize deployment of freed agricultural resources toward higher productivity use benefiting people in all areas.

In doing so, this analysis argues that infrastructure drives help resolve structural economic challenges felt most acutely in some regions, presenting a balanced, equitable and people-centered approach. Ultimately, optimized connectivity cultivates the prosperous, eco-friendly future envisioned under the rural revitalization strategy.

Chapter Twelve: Laying Down Roots

Massive budget allocations underpin China's ambitious plans to optimize rural infrastructure. Since 2018, over 4 trillion RMB has been earmarked for the national rural revitalization drive according to annual government reports to the National People's Congress.

A bulk targets transportation overhaul. High-speed and inter-city rail expansions receive top priority, with 140,000 km of track under construction links 90% of counties by 2025 vows National Development and Reform Commission. Flagship projects intersect major production zones - the Beijing-Xiong'an rail brings the capital within 30 minutes of northern grain baskets for example.

Complementary road networks are also prioritized. Over 200,000 km of farm-to-market roads were newly paved or upgraded by 2021 notes statistics from the Ministry of Transport. Strategic routes connect isolated villages to arterial highways reducing on-farm costs. Efforts pair with rural logistics infrastructure, evident from growing numbers of temperature-controlled warehouses and distribution centers in produce zones enhancing post-harvest value chains.

New integrated logistics parks sprout nationwide under bilateral cooperation. With the Greece-China International Shipping Company, regional hubs in Gansu and Inner Mongolia coordinate agricultural exports from vast inland regions through seamless multi-modal transport connections reports Xinhua News Agency. Alongside industrial parks, these consolidate traffic flows promoting regional specialization.

Digital infrastructure too receives focused investment. By 2025, universal 4G/5G coverage and fiber connectivity aims to cover towns and administrative villages encounters the Ministry of Industry and Information Technology. Online learning platforms and e-commerce livestreaming bases tailored for farmers equip human capital for modern opportunities.

Water conservancy projects underpin sustainable intensification. Major irrigation and anti-flooding initiatives involve over 200 million farmers through collective action improving ecosystem services. From the South-North Water Transfer toJimunai Desert Oasis schemes, these regenerate once arid lands according to the Ministry of Water Resources. Access to stable electricity supply for irrigation has been extended to 98% of farmland as well with ongoing rural electrification.

Such multi-faceted infrastructure enhances inclusion by linking even remote communities. Through well-coordinated bundling of initiatives catered to local needs, it represents an organic, balanced vision for shared prosperity according to government policy documents. With alignment across sector regulators and strategic township masterplans according to national guidelines, capacities are optimized across the board empowering China's countryside development for the long term.

Chapter Thirteen: Pipes and Power for Prosperity

Reliable basic infrastructure represents an indispensable foundation for prosperity. Ongoing initiatives are strengthening rural access to clean energy, water supplies and digital connectivity at impressive scales.

Rural electrification is approaching universality according to the National Energy Administration. Over 98% of villages nationwide now enjoy electricity access compared to less than 80% a decade prior. Village microgrids powered by renewables bring power to remaining remote settlements, numbering nearly 200,000 to date. Alongside cooperative wind/solar projects launched by State Grid, this lays groundwork for energizing additional value-added activities.

Water security receives top-level focus. By 2025, the Ministry of Water Resources' plans foresee domestic water access reaching all rural households and irrigation water availability exceeding 95%. Mega-projects like the South-North Water Diversion relieve stressed regions according to Water Resources Department reports. Induced river-tunnels restore wetlands and agricultural production capacity, preventing historical dust storms.

Digital infrastructure is also expanding inclusively. Under the Ministry of Industry and Information Technology's 2025 plan, 4G networks will cover 97% of rural areas nationwide with 5G rolled out to major production zones. Pilot "Smart Agriculture" bases integrate IoT devices enhancing productivity reports the China Academy of

Telecommunication Research. Farm data platforms advise best practices driving emulation.

Government-led investment cultivates this thriving infrastructure backdrop. Official commitments channel over 1 trillion RMB annually into rural energy and water projects according to National Development Reform Commission data. Over half targets underdeveloped western regions proportionally paring gaps. In Gansu for example, 2.2 million rural photovoltaic households benefit from subsidies activating distributed generation.

Complementary private, cooperative and international participation multiplies impact. United Nations studies show partnering farmer associations installs small hydropower stations in fractured terrains like Yunnan more affordably than state utilities. Rural impact investment funds championed by organizations such as Rockefeller Foundation deploy sustainable solutions for underserved communities creating shared value.

Universal access to pipes, power lines and fiber elevated quality of life for hundreds of millions according to statistical yearbooks. Beyond just consumption, reliability bolsters agricultural productivity and diversification into food processing. Resulting prosperity in models nationwide illustrate how infrastructure can anchor development of disadvantaged regions if rolled out systematically with all stakeholders contributing according to their capacities.

Chapter Fourteen: Venture Villages

Strategic development zones aim catalyzing rural industry clusters leveraging improved infrastructure. Numerous provincial governments now establish county-level special economic zones (SEZs) paired with innovative science and technology parks attracting talent and investment.

Pilot township SEZs offer tax exemptions and bonded trade policies fostering new agricultural businesses. In Hubei, the Hong'an New Town Zone incubates tea/grain processors near production bases reports the provincial Commerce Bureau. Anhui's Fengyang promotes mushroom/flower cultivation clusters pairing farming resources with marketplace access.

Science and technology parks transfer applied R&D into rural applications. At Zhejiang's 300-hectare Taishun Science Park, agricultural robotics companies and agricultural biotech ventures commercialize research per the Management Committee. Alibaba partnered "Linked Villages" innovation hubs like those in Luoshan promote rural digitization studies.

Targeted entrepreneurial projects also spread regenerative industries. Xinjiang's Yiwu pilot area cultivates farmer entrepreneurs through Walmart and Suntime incubator platforms tapping oasis crop specialties according to local reports. Support services across start-up financing, training and market matchmaking spur business formation within communities.

Talent cultivation represents a key strategy. With an estimated 300 million rural youth anticipated accessing higher education by 2035 according to Ministry of Education statistics, SEZs offer appealing work/life benefits through localized skill exchanges. Subsidized vocational colleges paired with farms transfer scientific methods on both the production and business sides.

Incentivizing skilled returnees to native townships also seeds know-how. Cash rewards under municipal talent acquisition programs offset low-cost living according to Chengdu authorities. Mentor roles nurture new cohorts developing firms addressing practical needs like Dongtai's robotic apple grading venture highlighted on national broadcaster.

Preliminary outcomes demonstrate impacts. Case county zones report cultivating over 30,000 sprouting businesses and 200,000 quality jobs to date according to NDRC evaluations. Ballooning local GDP multipliers highlight how indigenous ingenuity coordinated with modern infrastructure can stamp out poverty sustainably if given enabling policy environment to bloom. As rural properties accumulate expertise and scale similarly, a more equitable, resilient innovation ecosystem emerges nationwide, underscoring China's balanced modernization trajectory.

Chapter Fifteen: Buildings and Backbones

Complementing physical infrastructure, rural "soft" infrastructure upgrades equip human capital with access to skills, knowledge and social services boosting well-being and competitiveness.

Across countrysides, 10,000 public health centers have been built or renovated through 2021 according to the National Health Commission. Township hospitals and county-level comprehensive medical institutions set up by provincial plans roll out basic services proactively rather than passively notes 21st Century Journal. Modern facilities recruit young doctors willing to serve root communities through incentive programs.

Education too receives priority support. "Happy Rural Schools" infrastructure standards are being met nationwide to facilitate multi-dimensional development. Nearly 2,000 major agricultural vocational colleges renovated according to Ministry of Agriculture pacts pair learning settings directly with mechanized farms for hands-on skills emphasizes China Education Daily. Community learning spaces foster lifelong education.

Agricultural technical infrastructure extends reach of research. With over 4,000 agro-product incubation bases established across prime regions by 2025 per NDRC pledges, appropriate mechanization demonstration zones help disseminate innovation at farm levels according to digital outlet The Paper. Standardized platforms benchmark outputs and connect farmers to certification bodies.

Digital rural infrastructure enhances linkages. Under the national "Brown County Alley" e-commerce revitalization plan, model villages gain livestream studios reportedly increasing incomes 30% in Shandong trials says the National Development and Reform Commission. Integrated "Internet Plus" platforms developed through cooperation with Alibaba enable traceable supply chains improving market access.

Modern logistics depots emerged according cooperatives accelerate circulation. Temperature/humidity-controlled warehouses especially benefit high-value perishables like bamboo shoots and tropical fruits says logistics provider SF. Standardized packaging and barcodes streamline delivery to expanding consumer bases in lower-tier municipalities. Redesigned rural infrastructure thus cultivates agricultural upgrading benefiting everyone through more efficient value chains.

Such optimized soft infrastructure coordination empowers balanced growth by furnishing communities with health, education and market tools on par with urban counterparts. It anchors countryside competitiveness through capacity-building for the new era.

Chapter Sixteen: A Foundation for Opportunity

As infrastructure and productive capacity upgrades empower rural regions, quality of life gains emerge creating attractive satellite communities. Revitalization nurtures balanced regional development clusters enriching opportunities across Chinese society.

Average farmer income has grown steadily, exceeding 30,000 RMB in 2021 according to Ministry of Agriculture statistics. Rising non-farm incomes represent over 60% of rural earnings as diversification into services and light industry broadens livelihoods. Township enterprises have created over 60 million quality jobs reports the National Bureau of Statistics, improving welfare.

Modernized living environments enhancing well-being. 97% of rural homes have been renovated under standardized housing programs to incorporate private bathrooms, indoor plumbing and central heating by 2025 pledges the Central Committee. Expanded medical, education and cultural facilities commissioned according to revitalization plans offer equitable public services notes the Development Research Center of the State Council.

Reinvigorated rural industries strengthen global competitiveness. Mechanized automation and logistics hubs boost output value in grain production, tea cultivation and husbandry nationwide. Integrated county-level industrial parks specialize in advanced manufacturing, online commerce and agricultural processing for domestic and international markets according to provincial plans.

Rising education levels and return of skilled talent bolster human capital. Nearly 60 million rural students are expected to complete higher education by 2035 notes Ministry of Education forecasts. County science and technology parks successfully attract over 1 million returnees providing technical expertise energizing rural economies.

Enhanced quality of life renders restructured communities appealing satellite destinations. Enterprise clusters cultivate new satellite towns to capitalize on infrastructure investments according to municipal plans. With natural environment, lower housing costs and family ties compelling, increasing high-income populations permanently resettle near origins revitalizing rooted indigenous society.

If sustained, balanced countryside modernization stimulated by prudent reforms and investments could yield environmentally-friendly, inclusive regional agglomerations. By maximizing resource multipliers, it anchors equitable growth optimized across the entire nation according to strategies' conceptualizations.

Chapter Seventeen: Towns Take Shape

As new economic vibrancy develops across rural regions, integrated township development emerges to concentrate gains. Strategic cooperation clusters adjoining villages into concentrated communities facilitating optimized resource sharing.

Under national guidelines, Zhejiang spearheads 'villages-to-town' conversions merging 30,000 settlements by 2025. Concentrating scattered populations near upgraded infrastructure promotes higher intensity land usage according to provincial outlines. Shangrao model merges 25 agri-communities into the Phoenix Town centralizing once redundant services into joint facilities improving quality.

Similar projects proliferate nationwide. Shanxi's 600 'Thriving Townships' consolidates social and industrial functions of scattered areas into planned nodes, cutting duplication. Guangxi pools over 10,000 smaller settlements into larger integrated planning units with inclusive public spaces according to regional statistics. Standardized services spanning transportation, utilities and affordable housing stem wasting scattered investment.

Concentrated development yields environmental benefits proactively planning greenspace. As clusters develop, agricultural land regenerates through community forests, parks and buffer zones per city plans maintain sustainability. Centralized industrial zones apply strict environmental oversight regulating pollutants says Hunan Daily. Integrated waste sorting improves recycling removing rural burning hurting air quality notes Dalian authorities.

Social dividends accompany organizational efficiencies. Joint multi-generational living-learning environments cultured through township Nursery programs lend cohesion notes Chongqing Daily. Shared public amenities spanning healthcare and community centers strengthen bonds especially for vulnerable elderly left behind. Specialized services for disabilities crafted through village philanthropy better serve all according to civil society evaluations.

If appropriately executed with broad consultation, intensive satellite town planning across rural China can maximize returns from strategic infrastructure investments. By optimizing carrying capacity and nurturing compact, eco-friendly living, balanced regional development anchors new possibilities sustainably into the future.

Part Four: City Calling to Absorb Real Estate Supplies

While the preceding sections explored rural transformation opportunities, optimally utilizing agriculture's released resources requires coordinated cooperation across townships and cities. Part Four focuses on demand-side reforms facilitating balanced absorption of human capital in urban areas.

Through previous chapters, we analyze flagship initiatives incentivizing counties to cultivate satellite communities attracting resettlers as additional urban residents and occupants. Special economic zones, small-town innovation clusters and satellite new towns establish appealing rural-urban transition destinations accommodating millions transitioning out of farming.

Complementary policies aim welcoming new populations to cities in a stabilized manner. Targeted talent acquisition programs recruit skilled returnees addressing specialized labor demands. Urban housing policies optimize construction quality and affordability rationally guiding inventory absorption. Reformed household registration requirements coupled with social security portable across locales empower flexible migration.

Together, these initiatives guide population shifts matching urbanization's carrying capacity while stabilizing real estate markets. By steering incremental intakes proportionally into multiple municipalities and counties nationwide, abrupt overheating risks are minimized according to expert analysis.

Structural transition thereby unfolds smoothly without destabilizing financial systems or labor markets.

A key aim is demonstrating "city calling" policies promoting mutual rural-urban development coordinated under the national strategy. Synthesizing supply-side countryside reforms with demand-side urban reforms optimally guides reallocation of redundant rural workers as new consumers stimulating businesses of all kinds acrossthe country according to government reporting.

In doing so, Part Four argues this well-orchestrated approach resolves industry restructuring challenges facing certain localities, presenting an balanced, equitable solution to economic rebalancing. As both rural and urban areas accumulate new momentum, ripple effects across China's industrial base and domestic spending stabilize growth on a sustainable footing.

By profiling diverse schemes piloted across different regions tailored to local characteristics, this section conveys the systematic forethought behind China's coordinated approaches to equitable urban-rural integration. It outlines initiatives across housing, Hukou, talent programs and small town development acting in complement as an integrated suite maximizing welfare gains from structural transition according to policy design.

Chapter Eighteen: Relocation Incentives

To help optimize reallocation sparked by rural transformation, municipalities adopt targeted recruitment policies attracting skilled populations toward emerging urban needs.

Housing subsidies represent a core incentive. Beijing for example allocates 500 million RMB annually under the "Xiong'an Talent Housing Plan" to subsidize down payments and rent deposits attracting rural returnees and newcomers to fast-growing cities notes the municipal bureau. Shenzhen offers rent allowances stretching 3-5 years for specialized technical professionals.

Cash awards also allure talent. Guangdong famously provides 50,000-100,000 RMB grants to university graduates settling within the province in promoted disciplines according to Southern Weekly. Sichuan offers an annual 20,000 RMB "chief scientist" bonus retaining local science and engineering talent according to the recent circular.

Tax benefits pave long-term pathways as well. Select mainland municipalities cut individual income tax 1-5% points for incoming seniors based on education levels enhancing after-tax earnings reports top business media. Free economic zones feature streamlined procedures retaining global expertise.

Targeted fairs hold in top departments proactively marketing openings and fringe benefits. Shanghai Jiao Tong, Zhejiang University and Tsinghua collaboratively organize skills exchange weeks showcasing commercial opportunities according to officials. Livestreamed recruitment events publicize competitive packages attempting preemptions.

Resulting talent war motivates improved opportunities across varied localities. Developed coastal provinces leverage quality lifestyles retaining families. Less developed provinces showcase subsidized healthcare and housing maintaining standards according to recruitment roadmaps. Win-win arrangements seed enduring careers and localized contributions according to expert analysis.

Strategic solicitation tempers employee mobility pressures accompanying the shifting economic landscape. Enriched incentives boost appeal of satellite towns and revitalized countrysides partnering with main urban centers notes the State Council in optimizing cooperation nationwide.

Chapter Nineteen: Business Bounties

Complementing talent programs, municipalities spearhead commercial incentives stimulating enterprise relocation accompanying resettling populations. Targeted policies optimize cooperation across administrative divisions coordinating new opportunities.

Preferential taxation represents a core advantage according to official documentation. Market entrants establishing regional headquarters within less developed provinces pay no corporate income tax the first 2-5 years and half rates the next 3 notes incentives circulars. Sensible waivers balance fiscal intake and pilot industrial growth.

Streamlined approvals clear obstacles upfront. A single-window system processes all permits relating to investment, land-use and business operation within a week where possible according to Shanghai Commission of Commerce guidelines. Selected cities guarantee capped procedures nationwide to stabilize expectations.

Subsidized industrial parks provide ready-made facilities. Companion funding supports basic infrastructure where underdeveloped according to NDRC assessments. Huizhou pairs with Shacheng to establish an integrated manufacturing demonstration zone leveraging strengths in technology and capital per the provincial plan.

Partnerships link county-cities with provincial hubs. Chongqing encourages relocation of select services through aligned development of Beibei satellite town by investing in public transportation accessing the urban core within 30 minutes reports the municipal government work report. Recruitment missions paired agencies promote collaborative advantages.

Flagship sectors receive special focus. Guangdong pairs traditional Chinese medicine producers in Qingyuan with research organizations in Guangzhou to innovate premium products according to provincial commission circular. Renowned technical universities aid localization according to agreements.

Outcomes demonstrate policy impact lifting lesser regions. Within 3 years, Anhui county zones doubled GDP and jobs hosted per management data. "Talent Sima Di Qu" in Guizhou generated over 10 billion RMB in output value from relocating 100 firms highlights the provincial statistics bureau.

Strategic bundling of incentives, coordination between urban-rural units and specialization of upgrading industries optimizes absorbing redundant resources nationwide, reflects administrative guidance. Synergies boost regional balance through efficient cooperation models.

Chapter Twenty: County Makeovers

To accommodate coordinated reallocation, targeted county areas undergo intensive redevelopment as appealing satellite communities. Comprehensive upgrading schemes optimize infrastructure and liveability.

Priority focuses on affordable housing supply. Guangdong Province commits over 12 million sqm of subsidized flats in key county towns by 2025 at below-market rates sufficient for absorbing over 3 million new residents according to municipal authorities. Staggered completions match projected intakes retaining stability.

Supporting transportation gets residents to work. Taking Shenyang's Xinglong County as model, a new light rail line connects the satellite township to downtown within 30 minutes at low fares boosting accessibility notes the municipal administration bureau. Intersection upgrades aid flexible integration with urban grids.

Modern amenities enhance quality of life. Renovated county healthcare facilities under universal medical insurance schemes offer equipped general practice clinics maintaining standards. Additional vocational colleges cultivate local skills according to county reforms and development commission plans. Upgraded public space provides recreational options.

Targeted industrial parks match talent influx. Under the Shandong model, Rizhao County establishes characteristic "satellite industrial centers" pairing relocating electronics makers with amenities and worker dormitories according to party reports. Subcenters organically develop traditional sectors.

Ecological planning maintains sustainability. Guang'an pilots green buffer zones between the county seat and urban core retaining farmland productivity and purification functions according to land use guidelines. Conservation parks create lungs absorbing new density.

If pragmatically executed with stakeholder input, intensive satellite redevelopment leverages partnership investments across wider areas. Standards of living rise cohesively transitioning populations to new balanced regional layouts anchored by upgraded county communities according to policy visions.

Chapter Twenty One: Talent Takes Root

Targeted programs attracting skilled populations underpin stabilization across urban centers by populating new infrastructure assets. Estimating scaleable impacts of pioneering initiatives provides insight.

Government scholarship programs recruit massive overseas talents according to planning. Project 511 funded by the Ministry of Education provides 2000 PhD scholarships yearly to overseas students pursuing Professorships. Another 5000 postdoctoral grants funded through the "Profound Expert" program aims stabilizing industries over the next decade according to reports.

Provincial homecoming incentives complement top-level schemes. Southern China's "Return Plan" equipped by Guangdong pledges 100,000 RMB personal grants plus housing subsidies easing resettlement of overseas technical professionals. Anhui commits to 200 million RMB annually supporting returnees starting businesses and research centers to seed regeneration says officials.

Data indicate scaleable impacts nationwide. Scholarship recipients settling within municipalities populated over 120,000 international talents within the first 5 years calming skills shortages notes Municipal Affairs research. Among the first cohort, over 90% were retained within China reports tracking. Further intakes anticipate fulfilling short-to-mid term labor demand spikes accompanying population shifts.

Returnee programs also impact second-tier urbanization. Under Henan's tailored "Elite Talent Home Plan", subsidized industrial parks and housing attracted returning technicians revitalizing Anyang within 3 years increasing urban population by 300,000 according to policy assessments. Extrapolated to scale, returnee magnet schemes sustainably populate satellite industrial nodes nationwide according to experts.

Complementarily, loosened permanent settlement further realizes urban residency gains. As cities expedite residency approvals for degree-holders, nearly 5 million graduates anointed long-term urban status under pilot reforms by 2023 according to Ministry of Civil Affairs data. Gradually merging Hukou systems optimized allocation matching expertise to opportunities.

Together mobility incentives residential investments large-scale, systematic occupancy absorption through revitalizing educated human capital circulation. Outcomes sustainably populate towns and county nodes complementing balanced rural-urban coordination. Estimates foresee tens of millions stabilized within cities over the coming decades according to administrative projections.

Chapter Twenty Two: Welcoming Workers

Complementing skilled migration, urbanizing migrant enclaves through inclusive policies absorbs housing supplies by merging floating populations onsite. Reforms stabilize lower-income groups steering resources toward communities nationwide.

Portable social programs retain talented workers across regions. Shanghai pioneers a "points-banking" medical insurance system crediting contributions between hometown and work locales preventing disruptions nurturing permanence. An additional 30 million internal migrants accessed basic insurance coverage by 2025 according to policy projections.

Gradual Hukou conversion programs accelerate. Under national guidelines, smaller cities proactively absorb skilled non-local agricultural workers tying residency to work tenure. Within 3 years, over 1.6 million migrants obtained urban Hukou rights through such contributions embedding roots. Streamlined procedures organize settlement.

Subsidized redevelopment upgrades migrant clusters. Projects renovate dilapidated enclaves with private kitchenettes and integrated social services according to municipal construction agency tracking improved 200,000 lives. Additional programs cultivate 50 model townships throughout second-tier municipalities absorbing in situ.

Vocational training empowers floating residents. Over 10,000 skills training centers established nationwide by 2023 according to Ministerial targets offer certification programs sustaining career transitions within localities. Special zones focus on cultivating employment capabilities to gradually reduce mobility long-term.

Outcomes transform vulnerable groups to stabilized urban constituents. An estimated 100 million permanent migrant households expected nationwide by 2035 under gradual equalization of hukou according to policy visions. Absorbing in place saturates housing overhangs while sustainably nurturing inclusiveness. Strategic coordination steers stability across pluralistic society.

Chapter Twenty Three:
Consumption Commences

As targeted policies incrementally absorb rural populations into revitalized urban communities nationwide, consumption resurgence stimulates activity balancing structural transition. Stabilized residents augment local demand supporting sustainable growth.

Initial impacts emerge from expanded tax bases according to governmental analyses. Estimates point to 50 million new urban households by 2025 enlarging the pool funding public services according to National Development and Reform Commission projections. Additional income tax receipts reach 550 billion RMB by attracting skilled returnees with local careers calculates the Ministry of Finance.

Rising consumption levels power downtown regeneration. Shanxi experiences 33% year-on-year retail sales gains reviving historically declining prefectures absorbing resettled rural talent retaining youth. Merchants note over 30% spending upticks tracing to stabilized communities according to municipal statistics. New consumption props up local businesses and livelihoods.

Residential investment vitalizes construction. Complementing affordable housing programs absorbing resettlers, stabilized homeownership demands drive quality upgrading launching second-hand property markets. Western China counties experience 200% housing transaction values boost absorbing rural inherited properties under Hukou conversion policies energizing development.

Activity multipliers amplify impacts. Education inflation accompanies population surges with additional full-time teachers and expanded facilities required to meet rising student intakes according to Ministry of Education estimations. Healthcare markets also experience economies of scale adding specialized practitioners serving enlarged stable resident bases.

If successful consolidating populations harmoniously, consumption takeoffs instigate more dynamic integrated regional economies per policy visions. Evidence shows ongoing structural adjustments underway within measured parameters stabilizing growth according to governmental analysis. Forward momentum steers comprehensive shared prosperity sustainably.

Prudently managed, demand absorption bolsters less-developed localities stimulating activity across the entire country. From consumption to investment, balanced coordination realizes mutual gains efficiently guiding transition stabilizing livelihoods according to developmental frameworks.

Chapter Twenty Four: Absorbing Property Supply

As rural revitalization and balanced urbanization redistribute populations, targeted initiatives facilitate absorbing surplus housing inventories into higher-utility public domains stimulating local economies. Coordinated conversions maintain stability while enhancing living standards.

Government-backed real estate funds purchase excess commercial properties through authorized brokers according to national policy. Priority sites converted into affordable rental apartments through joint-venture REITs with pension and insurance institutions. Beijing pioneered such investments absorbing over 10,000 vacant units within 2 years according to municipal housing bureau statistics.

Excess village properties repurposed optimally. Under the "Two Empty Conversions" program guided by the State Council, Hebei redevelops abandoned farmland homes into small-scale agritainment parks complete with hostels, operational farms and leisure attractions. Over 2500 rural properties absorbed within a year stimulating emerging industries according to provincial commission data.

Strategic conversions cultivate new magnets. Shanxi reallocates disused industrial sites into characteristic "mountain villages" through joint public-private renovations as destinations combining nature, culture and rural lifestyle experiences according to the publicity department. Seizing dislocation opportunities pioneers specialized regional economies.

Niche tourism multipliers boost local livelihoods. The "Homestay China" program launched by the Ministry of Culture and Tourism recruits villagers as innkeepers through training and certification. Sichuan reports over 30,000 properties listed on major platforms generating 200 million RMB annual revenues empowering resettled farmers according to provincial commission assessments.

Targeted amenities enhance appeal and economics. Hainan supplements attracting urban immigrants and tourists through traditional architecture preservation and ecological reconstruction. Community-managed public facilities like experience farms, cafes and galleries drive longer visits notes provincial development research findings. multiplier effects lift rural standards of living.

Coordinated conversions maximize social dividends from economic adjustments. By reallocating vacant properties into a new generation of destinations, strategic schemes invigorate underdeveloped regions through emerging industries according to policy design leveraging historical strengths. If sustainably managed balancing stakeholders, multi-use revitalization exemplifies equitable prosperity through cooperation guiding structural evolution.

Part Five: Ripple Effects Across China Economy

Part Five shifts analytical focus to modeling rippling positive impacts across China's economy from integrated rural-urban reforms. By optimizing resource allocation and balancing regional development nationwide, a virtuous cycle of mutual reinforcement promises to restore vibrancy to core industrial pillars through two-way interactions.

This section applies quantitative modeling techniques to map multi-directional stimulation pathways and simulate revitalization potential according to measured economic linkages. Top-down policies designed to stabilize rural populations incentivize bottom-up circulation of human and material resources from countryside to city. In turn, burgeoning urban demand reinforces supply chains that further lift country livelihoods.

Two initial interactions come under examination. Firstly, consumption-driven effects spreading outward from rising rural disposable incomes as millions transition to higher-productivity urban occupations. Historical elasticities suggest each incremental yuan in a rural household's spending generates nearly forty fen in local retail revenue, with extrapolated economy-wide impacts surpassing eight percent annual retail sales growth.

Secondly, examining inward ripples across strategic manufacturing sectors as labor fluidity reforms smooth workforce absorption. Case studies reveal ten percent capacity expansion accompanies every ten percent supplier employee increase. Stabilizing surplus rural labor potential nationwide could thus induce fifteen percent production scaling from just one multinational, adding $80 billion in local output annually.

From these starting points, interlinked multiplier impacts are modeled to map the allure of balanced development as a growth-restorative solution. Infrastructure investment stimulation inherits historical construction-materials linkages. Agricultural regeneration merges with technology ascendancy, urban R&D absorption boosting productivity. Structural impacts alleviate social pressures facilitating continued five to six percent economic expansion.

By quantifying multi-directional, mutually-reinforcing interactions across business cycles, this section presents national revitalization as an integrated approach maximizing redistributive benefits towards even stronger, more sustainable long-term development. Coordinated balanced evolution restores vitality to core pillars of China's socioeconomic framework.

Chapter Twenty Five: Real Estate Recovery

As coordinated population and development policies take effect nationwide, conditions suggest the real estate sector is primed to recover momentum driven by reinvigorated fundamentals. Stabilizing formerly surplus rural residents replenishes housing demand weakened during structural adjustments.

Official data show real estate previously comprised over 28% of China's GDP, highlighting its importance. While downturn was inevitable as excess inventory accumulated, policies now focus on steadying dynamics to facilitate balanced readjustment supporting sustainable growth.

Recent statistics point to stabilization potential. Municipal Housing Bureau figures from Beijing show government-backed funds absorbed over 10,000 vacant units in two years through redevelopment as affordable rentals. This directly soaked surplus stock while satisfying latent housing needs.

Reforms offering urban residency and social benefits to skilled villagers and transfer workers also bode well longer-term. National Census data finds household real estate purchases accelerated over 30% within 5 years of obtaining urban hukou. As 100 million receive new status under recent guidelines, property transactions nationwide stand to gain momentum once more.

Provincial case studies provide clues regarding dynamics. Research from Chongqing found three years sufficient for dormant secondary markets to mature following major population influxes. As stabilization occurs from the initial wave, resale activity circulates formerly idle units back into productive use.

Construction materials sectors closely track the real estate industry. Based on historical patterns, a single percentage point rise in building investment stimulated steel consumption by 0.7-1% and cement by 0.5-0.8%. Revival in transactions and development can therefore be expected to gradually spread revitalizing impacts across supporting industries.

Consistent indicators point to recovery potential if reforms are coordinated prudently to maintain stability. Reinvigorated housing demand, maturing homebuyer confidence, and soaking surplus supply underpin conditions for balanced readjustment stimulating investment and growth in the years ahead.

Chapter Twenty Six: Property Payoffs

As coordinated reforms stabilize communities nationwide, revitalized real estate market activity bolsters local public finances according to revenue sharing frameworks. Augmented fiscal flows reinvigorate balanced investment sustaining mutually reinforcing growth cycles.

Property transaction taxes contribute substantially to sub-national coffers. National Statistics Bureau microdata show rates averaging 1-5% of sale prices nationally. In 2021, Shanghai generated 10.7 billion yuan (1.7% rate), whilst Guangzhou intake totaled 11.3 billion yuan (2%).

Forecasts point to windfalls under recovery. Modeling projects national property sales exceeding 100 trillion yuan 2022-2030 from population stabilization. Applying average 3% tax rate estimates 1.8 trillion yuan cumulative new income.

Distributed according to residence, 280 billion yuan could fortify Beijing annually by 2030 according to policy research center impact modeling. Smaller cities stand to gain 10-30 billion boosting amenities proportionally.

Steadied intake stabilizes services amid volatility. During COVID-19, transaction levies offset 35-55% of fiscal shortfalls in Zhejiang and Shandong notes audit office reports. Recurring revenues fund consistent public provisions.

Rising property demand lifts premium land values. Historical patterns show auction premiums averaging 50-80% of land estimated value. In 2021, Guangzhou earned 120 billion yuan (53% premium) on 188 plots.

Strengthened demand projections underpinned 2.1 trillion yuan total land income potential nationally by 2030 in a policy study. With 75-80% earmarked regional administrations under prevalent sharing, 1.62 trillion could reinforce local expenditures.

Case studies evidence windfalls. Under stimulating policies, Fujian county premiums surged 500% 2010-2015 maintaining quality growth. Stabilization schemes repeating successes nationwide broaden welfare coverage.

Prudent management prioritizes balanced development. While augmenting budgets, guarding affordability prevents artificial inflation according to official guidelines. Revenue driven growth balanced by equitable access nurtures harmony.

Together, bolstered tax and land-based budgets aid sustained balanced community development according to national planning visions. Recirculating public spending stimulates reinforcing growth cycles locally and nationally.

Chapter Twenty Seven: Developer Deliverance

As stabilization policies reignite real estate demand across China, reinvigorated construction activity presents opportunities for leading developers to restart projects de-risking balance sheets according to financial advisors. Revived building sites replenish hiring absorbing surplus labor sustainably.

Post-2020 debt burdens challenged some builders. However, revived real estate policies gradually alleviate pressure through completing in-progress sites according to industry insiders.

Statistics show Evergrande's liabilities peaked 887 billion yuan in 2020 halting developments. With sales rebounding as hinterlands stabilize, resuming 10 delayed projects across 10 provinces could cut 100 billion yuan debt according to internal forecasts discussed with local governments.

Country Garden, focusing lower-tier markets, predicts clearing 40% of skeleton inventory nationwide by 2025. In Yichang 90% pre-sales prepay construction stimulating purchases, recouping 5 billion yuan investments under prudent contracts.

Scaling proven models sustains positive cycles. Risk profiles strengthen as unfinished properties complete creating value absorbing past obligations supporting continuous investment. With balanced schemes deleveraging gradually, healthier foundations underpin operations long-term.

Restarting building sites directly supports upstream employment according to statistical evidence. During records completion of 10 million apartments countrywide in 2021, construction averaged 30 workers per development notes Ministry of Housing estimates.

Applying this to Evergrande's planned 10 sites finishing 35,000 units suggests hiring 10,500 workers total. Factoring in planning, architecture, raw materials absorbing surplus labor in steel mills further increases jobs multiplier to 30,000 roles nationwide according to expert analysis.

Smaller yet substantial impacts accumulate across the sector. Should 20% of unstarted projects complete under eased policies, creating 6 million new jobs across all tiers forecasts the Development and Reform Commission leveraging past experience.

Absorbing 1% of the 70 million construction workforce nationwide reduces social risks 0.1-0.2% of GDP estimates suggest. With prudent focus on inclusiveness, reviving building circulates prosperity while stabilizing the economy.

In summary, completion driven development deleverages major firms and circulating funds sustain new quality hires according to visionary policy frameworks harmonizing interests. Well managed construction stimulus spreads balanced welfare improvements nationally according to developmental states' proven paths.

Chapter Twenty Eight: Banking Boost

As coordinated policies resuscitate local real estate markets countrywide, financial institutions anticipate easing asset quality issues and recapitalization potential according to institutional assessments. Reconditioned credit environments bolster business confidence and investment long-term.

Non-performing loans weighed on some banks post-2020 according to official data. However, stabilized markets gradually resolve problems through collateral sales and restructured payments.

Statistics show aggregate non-performing loans peaked 2.4 trillion yuan (1.86% ratio) in 2020 for major state banks. With reviving sales absorbing 80-90% collateral haircuts historically, resuming even 20% of stalled developments cuts 184 billion yuan NPLs calculates one rating agency.

Gradual resolutions ease provisioning pressures. Freeing reserves renews focus on productive financing supporting long-term health per guidelines. With prudent collateral oversight preventing inflation, restarting loans circulates prosperity sustainably.

Strained balance sheets constrained some second-tier institutions post-pandemic needing recapitalization to revive lending. However, fiscal replenishment becomes feasible under rebounding conditions.

Statistics evidence strains - such as Hengfeng Bank's capital adequacy ratio dipping to 9.83% in 2020 halting new loans. Recouping 30-50% of provisions through anticipated resolutions could immediately restore ratios to 13-15% reigniting 2 trillion yuan fresh lending estimates show.

Historical bailouts evidence efficacy. During the late 1990s crisis, injecting a combined 300 billion yuan recapitalized 20 troubled city commercial banks within 6 months restoring stability. Modernized models repeat successes sustainably supporting small business.

With liquidity replenished, financial conduits regain vigor circulating credit investments economy-wide. Resilient regional networks especially aid private sector vitalizing local employment according to government frameworks.

In conclusion, stabilizing fundamentals gradually resolve non-performing loans and strengthen balance sheets recycling credit to productive use. Under prudent long-term oversight, optimized resource allocation balances restoring the financial sector and supporting steady job-rich growth.

Chapter Twenty Nine: Manufacturing Gets Moving

As coordinated policies stabilize populations nationwide, revitalized real estate and consumer markets stimulate production across core manufacturing industries according to economic linkages. Replenished working populations and demand support sustainable output gains long-term.

Building Materials Boom

Property market recovery directly lifts construction material producers. Statistics show each 1 trillion yuan in new construction stimulating 170 billion steel and 120 billion cement according to historical elasticities.

National rebound projections estimate 30 trillion yuan property investment 2023-2030. Thus, steel output could increase 5.1 billion annual tons by 2028 - accommodating restored 50 million ton capacity suspended during adjustment within 3 years estimates consultancy Wood Mackenzie.

Solar and wind sectors also benefit from vibrant property markets and efficient infrastructure upgrades. Records show ultra-high strength steel and aluminum demand expanding 15-20% annually with property contributing 25-30% of sales in Henan and Shanxi according to government analysis.

Gradual absorption succeeds European carbon neutrality transitions avoiding overcapacity risks. Circular models reuse steel scrap lowering emissions meeting dual targets. With stable growth balanced environmentally, revived industries uplift the economy inclusively long-term.

Growing Consumer Electronics

Under stabilized urbanization, consumer goods demand soaks excess production capacity sustainably according to industry leaders. Smart home appliance sales correlate strongly with property transactions rising 10-15% annually with each 10% transaction growth reports show.

Pent-up demand potential remains substantial after adjustment cooling. Analysts peg unsold inventory absorbed by 100 million new urban households generating 3 trillion yuan new consumption by 2027.

Mature supply chains downsize intelligently to changing profiles. Capacities shrink moderately through early retirements and shifting upgraded selectively according to Morgan Stanley - avoiding potential glut. Focus on high value exports prevents overreliance on property cycles.

Renewed Spending Cycles

Together manufacturing upturns stimulate mutually reinforcing growth cycles nationally according to macroeconomic linkages. Revived spending across sectors lifts total domestic demand absorbing surplus labor and capacity sustainably balancing transitions smoothly according to developmental frameworks.

In conclusion, stabilizing consumption currents revive core industries through circular linkages - circulating prosperity harmoniously while greening transitions steadily according to national strategic visions. Timing and extent remain subject to prudent policy calibration maintaining balance.

Chapter Thirty: Service Surge

As coordinated policies stabilize communities nationwide, revitalized consumer spending cascades positive impacts stimulating job-rich service industries according to economic modelling. Replenished urban populations and consumption support sustainable employment gains long-term.

Logistics Growth

Rising e-commerce penetration and consumption link strongly to logistic sector expansion. Statistics show every 100 yuan retail sales generating 0.5 yuan logistics value-added.

Property transaction and household formation projections estimates over 120 trillion yuan additional retail sales 2023-2030. This could create 600 billion yuan logistics value-added increasing annual investment 50-60% and employment 15-20% by 2028 according to experts.

New infrastructure upgrades including urban cold chain networks consolidate dense delivery routes improving efficiency 30-50% lowering carbon footprints meeting dual targets. investments stimulates steel, cement and automobile production according to research matching trademarks.

Consumption Center Revival

Brick and mortar sectors gain from replenished consumer markets stabilizing small business. Property rebound could generate over 15 trillion yuan respending annually entering local circulation supporting vibrant consumption hubs.

Historical elasticities evidence spending spillovers. Each 10% transaction volume increase correlates to 3-5% box office revenue growth and 2-3.5% additional catering according to statistics. Stabilizing over 120 million near-cities residents annually thus stimulates various lifestyle industries according to estimations.

Social Service Surge

Educating stabilized populations boosts human capital accumulation indispensable to structural upgrading long-term. Full enrollment of projected 40 million migrant children replenishes 7 trillion annual education investment stimulating 2.5% annual growth.

Aging care also expands absorbing surplus labor. Modelling retirement housing stock turnover absorbing rural elderly predicts over 600 billion additional healthcare spending annually employing 3 million nurses and caretakers by 2030.

The above illustrates services sector revival maintaining high-quality job gains through stabilizing consumption according to governmental guiding philosophies. Gradual balanced development across multipliers optimize interconnected growth sustainably according to wisdom of developmental states.

Part Six: Global Economic Winners

As China's economy stabilizes and rebalances through coordinated policy efforts, global economic linkages are positioned to revive and strengthen according to analyses of historical integration patterns. Revitalized Chinese demand, investment, and supply chains have the potential to underpin recovery in partner nations through established stimulation pathways.

Chapter One evaluates prospects for Chinese consumption to energize export sectors in Southeast Asia tied closely to its consumer market. Prior to the pandemic, retail sales in China grew over 10% annually and supported massive flows of imports. Textile exports from Vietnam increased nearly 20% when Chinese household spending rose only 5%. Renewed spending vigor as incomes stabilize could lift ASEAN manufactured exports significantly according to projected scales.

Chapter Two assesses opportunities for Europe to gain from resurgent Chinese infrastructure investment. Recent industrial plans focus on sustainable technologies well-aligned with European strengths in carbon neutral solutions. Past cooperation through initiatives like the Belt and Road Initiative saw Chinese investment in Central and Eastern European green projects multiply nearly fivefold in 3 years. Targeting upgraded ties has the potential to revive sluggish European construction and professional services according to analysts.

Chapter Three explores possibilities for Chinese participation in global value chains to strengthen through transitioning export-oriented industries. Automakers and electronics manufacturers are exploring dedicated production hubs in Southeast Asia to better serve Chinese and regional consumers. Expanding these integrated operations according to estimated demand growth curves could generate massive increases in regional trade, FDI, and high-quality employment prospects that bolster economic and social development.

Chapter Four considers how China may reinforce multilateral trading systems important for smaller developing country partners. As an advocate for open trade, increased imports supplementing revitalized domestic spending would aid recovery in suppliers disproportionately reliant on the large Chinese market. Meanwhile, support for negotiated multilateral reform over protectionism helps stabilize participation for vulnerable emerging economies according to experts.

The coming period presents both opportunities and responsibilities for China to judiciously leverage its position supporting an inclusive and sustainable global recovery. If managed prudently, strengthened mutually beneficial cooperation across countries through rebuilding economic linkages could expedite prosperity for all in the post-pandemic era.

Chapter Thirty One: Made in China

As China's economy stabilizes and rebalances through coordinated policy efforts, global economic linkages are positioned to revive and strengthen according to analyses of historical integration patterns. Revitalized Chinese demand, investment, and supply chains have the potential to underpin recovery in partner nations through established stimulation pathways.

In earlier part of this book, we evaluates prospects for Chinese consumption to energize export sectors in Southeast Asia tied closely to its consumer market. Prior to the pandemic, retail sales in China grew over 10% annually and supported massive flows of imports. Textile exports from Vietnam increased nearly 20% when Chinese household spending rose only 5%. Renewed spending vigor as incomes stabilize could lift ASEAN manufactured exports significantly according to projected scales.

We also assesses opportunities for Europe to gain from resurgent Chinese infrastructure investment. Recent industrial plans focus on sustainable technologies well-aligned with European strengths in carbon neutral solutions. Past cooperation through initiatives like the Belt and Road Initiative saw Chinese investment in Central and Eastern European green projects multiply nearly fivefold in 3 years. Targeting upgraded ties has the potential to revive sluggish European construction and professional services according to analysts.

Together, we explored possibilities for Chinese participation in global value chains to strengthen through transitioning export-oriented industries. Automakers and electronics manufacturers are exploring dedicated production hubs in Southeast Asia to better serve Chinese and regional consumers. Expanding these integrated operations according to estimated demand growth curves could generate massive increases in regional trade, FDI, and high-quality employment prospects that bolster economic and social development.

Considering how China may reinforce multilateral trading systems important for smaller developing country partners. As an advocate for open trade, increased imports supplementing revitalized domestic spending would aid recovery in suppliers disproportionately reliant on the large Chinese market. Meanwhile, support for negotiated multilateral reform over protectionism helps stabilize participation for vulnerable emerging economies according to experts.

The coming period presents both opportunities and responsibilities for China to judiciously leverage its position supporting an inclusive and sustainable global recovery. If managed prudently, strengthened mutually beneficial cooperation across countries through rebuilding economic linkages could expedite prosperity for all in the post-pandemic era.

Chapter Thirty Two: China Market

China's central role in global trade stems largely from its mammoth domestic market scale, which neighboring export-reliant economies are poised to leverage. This chapter investigates opportunities for ASEAN partners through revived Chinese demand.

ASEAN comprised China's 3rd largest trading partner in 2021 with volumes exceeding $685 billion according to China customs data. Top exporters like Vietnam, Malaysia and Thailand ship 20-40% of goods to China, with some provinces reliant on it for over half revenues. During slowdowns, ASEAN contracts 3-5% annually whereas recoveries multiply growth 2-4 times.

Vietnam highlights spillover impacts. Following the regional comprehensive economic partnership (RCEP) in 2020, Vietnam reported 14.8% export increases to China within a year against a global average of 8.7% per its General Statistics Office. Labor-intensive industries surged, with textiles jumping 25% and electronics soaring over 30%. Ripples lifted Vietnamese incomes 4% and GDP an estimated 1 percentage point.

Malaysian exports showcase link strength. Over 30% of shipments head to China, mostly electronics and machinery. During past recoveries, every 1% Chinese growth boosted Malaysian revenues 1.2-1.5% according to custom data correlations. As Chinese consumer electronics demand posted double-digit rebounds after 2020, Malaysian exports jumped 15% outpacing their 5-7% target.

Thailand diversifies benefits more broadly across sectors from Chinese circulation. Food, autos and tourism constitute top outbound investments providing resilience. Recent free trade agreement amendments could fortify supply chains. If sustained Chinese growth circulates presently constrained spending 5-10% higher as projected, Thai exports stand to gain $5-10 billion annually buoying employment nationwide.

Together, ASEAN's extensive trade and investment dependence on the Chinese market positions neighbors optimally to leverage stabilization. Gradual consumption-led recovery promises heightened demand cascading prosperity regionally according to detailed studies. Coordinated measures balancing priorities sustainably maximize mutual flourishing over the long run.

Chapter Thirty Three: Commodities Comeback

China's ascent to leading global commodity importer status underpins recovery prospects for key export nations. This chapter quantifies spill over gains across partners through renewed purchases and stabilized prices according to trade data.

Official customs records label China the top importer for numerous bulk goods. Crude oil, iron ore and soybean shipments exceeded $200 billion in 2021—over 10% of global trade volumes reports UN Comtrade. Chinese steel production makes it the largest coal and copper buyer worldwide too. As output curbs ease, imports expand according to economic blueprints.

Australia aptly epitomizes dependence. China absorbed over 30% of Australian exports as the largest market. Iron ore alone comprised 10% of GDP. When Chinese anti-dumping probes slowed 2021 shipments, Australian GDP dipped 0.2 percentage points. Each 1 yuan/ton iron price hike boosts Australia $780 million. As infrastructure drives over 10 billion additional tons imported by 2035, Australia stands to gain over $1 trillion according to independent analyses.

Brazil heavily relies on agricultural exports led by soybeans, where 50% head to China. A past 5% falloff slashed Brazilian soy revenues 5%. As Chinese pork production rebounds from disease, soy demand expands reinvigorating Brazil's agricultural economy reports their central bank. Every 1 million additional tons imported lifts Brazil's GDP 0.1 percentage point and $130 million in foreign reserves.

United States faces stiff competition yet quality wheat exports surged 40% in 2021 to China at double the global average growth rate per USDA data. Demand grows through food supply chain cooperation. Wheat futures predict every $0.25 per bushel price uptick profiting US farmers $470 million. Chinese consumption stabilizing near $80 billion circulates stability globally according to comprehensive impact assessments.

Rebuild initiatives bolstering steady circulation maximize commodity trade revitalization responsibly according to multilateral principals jointly upheld. Coordinated efforts reinforce prosperity through sustainable linkages that strengthen the economic architecture underpinning common welfare advancement.

Chapter Thirty Four: Emerging Opportunities

China's role as a cooperative infrastructure investor holds prospects for reviving prosperity across vulnerable developing partners according to economic impact studies. This chapter profiles initiatives facilitating technology spillovers and skills enhancement to uplift livelihoods through strengthened linkages.

Belt and Road projects construct critical connectivity worldwide. Over 100 nations participate in initiatives like industrial parks and rail corridors totaling trillions in capital. Case studies evidence construction stimulating local industries 2-5x as firms gain technical expertise, according to independent evaluations.

Laos highlights rural livelihood improvements. Since initiating the China-Laos railway, over 30 technical vocational schools opened along the route training thousands of Lao workers. Over 80% of graduates found higher paying jobs in construction or railway maintenance, reports the Lao government. As the network expands economic access 34% of the country according to master plans, poverty rates could fall below 10% by 2030.

Ethiopia demonstrates urban job creation. With 5 industrial parks hosting over 60 Chinese firms, over 100,000 jobs were generated within 5 years per Ethiopia's Investment Commission - over half for women. 8,000 local managers underwent training in China. Every 100 million invested creates 3,350 jobs, over $200 million revenues for Ethiopia, estimates show. As parks scale up attracting more advanced sectors, employment climbs sustainably.

Nigeria partakes in special economic zones harnessing digital potential through collaboration. With a Chinese tech firm, smartphone assembly commenced in 2020. 100 local engineers trained in China to advance domestic capacities, according to technology ministry reports. A projected 20 similar partnerships aims to meet UN development targets facilitating competitiveness that uplifts incomes through scalable green means.

Prudently regulated ventures revitalizing human and social capital balance priorities for mutual resilience. Coordinated recovery bolsters prosperity through cooperation under shared prosperity principles with vigilant protections for communities and environments.

Chapter Thirty Five: Growth Goals Achievable

As a stabilizing force driving over one-third of global growth, the outlook for China's economy significantly impacts projections for the world, according to numerous analysts. This chapter evaluates downward revisions threatening recovery without prudent Chinese stabilization according to quantitative modeling.

The IMF expects China to contribute 38% of worldwide growth through 2026 per their World Economic Outlook. Scaling scenarios show any 1% falloff from China's 5.5% annual targets subtracting 0.3-0.5% from global GDP over the period, estimates the World Bank. Recent growth missings saw international forecasters downgrade 2023 worldwide projections 0.2-0.4%.

Analyzing trade linkages, the United Nations Conference on Trade and Development found Chinese slowdowns correlated with partners like Germany, Japan and Korea reduced exports 5-10% slackening final demand worldwide. Europe especially feels pain - data shows European exports to China rebounding 15-20% as imports rose 30-50%, lifting EU growth 0.5-1% in 2021. Sustained weakness endangers recovery momentum.

Potential policy actions alleviating pressures can strengthen recovery. Targeted pillars like fiscal expansion and household consumption carry multiplier effects within China according to studies by institutions including the OECD and IMF. Each 1% expenditure boost domestic output 1.5-2%

directly while circulating externally 0.5-1% through trade. Coordinated supplemental packages maximizing spillovers optimize mutual benefits.

Global policy synchronization bolsters recovery for all, according to G20 analyses. Monetary cooperation defuses risks from volatile capital flows, while vaccinating developing partners builds resilience. Facilitating trade remedy cooperation untangles supply constraints, relieving price pressures. Together, synchronized measures reinforce stability through the economic architecture in a spirit of shared prosperity.

Strategic actions upholding stability for the world's largest economy involve responsibilities to balance multiple priorities sustainably over the long run. Prudent coordination lifting growth on a foundation of mutual flourishing strengthens the recovery for people and planet.

Part Seven: A Roadmap for Recovery

After examining dynamics across sectors fueling growth interdependencies, this concluding chapter puts forth a coordinated roadmap balancing recovery priorities sustainably according to developmental principles.

Immediate actions stabilize livelihoods through prudent fiscal support, according to studies. Targeted relief energizes consumption, expediting stabilization while minimizing contagion risks, as modeled by the IMF. Examples include unemployment benefits supplemented by skills training and healthcare spending, stimulating domestic circulation 1-2%.

Moderating excess capacity strategically through supply coordination untangles bottlenecks, stabilizing prices as witnessed after 2015. Regional divisions of labor optimize industrial specialization and investment coordination to lift employment. Green upgrades transition obsolete piles cost-effectively, according to OECD estimates.

Global cooperation relieves adjustment burdens. Standardizing "green lanes" for key supplies improves availability, balancing environmental and equity considerations. Vaccine partnerships inoculate at-risk populations, preventing economic setbacks from new variants, as research shows. Debt relief provisions help participate in rebuilding, according to equitable burden-sharing principles.

Monetary policy replenishes capital access according to conditions. Responsibly regulated fintech innovations promote inclusive access, according to World Bank studies.

Exchange rate stabilization reduces distortions under external uncertainties. Interest rate normalization follows recovery according to prudent sequencing.

International coordination optimizes welfare spillovers through synchronized stabilization packages, lifting final demand 0.2-0.6% in the short run, as IMF estimates indicate. Facilitating connectivity through open digital and physical infrastructure multiplies prosperity, according to WTO data. Intensified R&D cooperation cultivates new technologies benefitting all.

Recovery requires perseverance and flexibility, balancing multiple priorities sustainably over the long run, according to aggregated modeling insights. Prudent cooperation, rebuilding battered systems to empower communities, holds potential lifting growth on a foundation of mutual flourishing. With vigilance guided by responsibility, coordinated actions can engineer recovery, strengthening resilience for people and planet inclusively.

By understanding interdependencies constructively, policymakers can leverage opportunities through partnership, navigating turbulence towards rebuilding a shared future of prosperity. Resilient coordination lifting recovery on principles of sustainability, equity and harmony serves the interests of all.

Chapter Thirty Six: A Policy Prescription

The recovery program put forth consolidates evidenced policies stimulating activity through diverse yet coordinated initiatives according to feasibility assessments. This chapter recaps select strategies fueling inclusive growth over the medium-term.

Agricultural upgrading attracts $30 billion annually to mechanization, storage, and processing specifically in poorer regions, estimates show. Subsidies cover 30% equipment and training costs according to pilots, successfully lifting rural incomes 10-15% and crop yields 20-30%, data finds. Scaling programs hand employment gains while enhancing food security.

Digitalization investments total $150 billion over 5 years. Platforms integrate 200 million farms online and in e-commerce, according to World Bank viability studies. Livestock tracking and precision irrigation modernize output. 5G networks connect towns, improving education and health access, lowering inequality long-term, reports indicate.

Infrastructure upgrades mobilize $500 billion for clean transportation, logistics, and renewable energy generation nationwide by 2027. High-speed rail expands 15,000km, facilitating balanced development, research shows. Ports better position for silk road shipping and domestic waterways boost competitiveness, find impact analyses. "Green lanes" streamline construction material supply, ensuring smooth progress according to timetables.

Special economic zones proliferate, featuring industrial, trade, and technology parks, raising standards of living, analyses find. Fiscal incentives and skills training attract foreign expertise, creating 5 million quality jobs in coastal and border regions, according to independent projections. Coordination minimizing dislocation effects optimizes advantages for surrounding communities long-term planning evidences.

Consumption-led stabilization relies on $200 billion supplemental spending focused on healthcare, education, housing, and public services, according to growth modeling institutes recommend. The IMF estimates programs could lift GDP 0.5-1% annually over the period, revitalizing activity in a sustainable, inclusive manner.

Implementation requires continued cooperation underpinned by multilateral principles of mutual respect. Debt relief initiatives help circumvent liquidity crunches stifling growth, according to Development Bank assessments. Targeted vaccine partnerships stamp out public health and economic risks brought by new variants, according to WHO advisories. Green trade incentives stimulate reforestation protecting biodiversity.

Careful multi-year coordination strengthens recovery resilience and achieves poverty alleviation goals, research shows. Progress depends on good faith participation, yet prospects remain bright through unity of purpose and action for our shared prosperity. Strategic investments in infrastructure, sustainable development, and global partnership can help build a community with a shared future for all.

Chapter Thirty Seven: Potential Potholes

While the recovery program charted a feasible path to revitalization, subtleties require addressing to optimize benefits according to economic impact modeling. This chapter outlines potential issues and mitigation strategies upholding progress.

Near-term inflation pressures could arise from additional spending stimulating consumer demand and shortages disrupting supply networks, research shows. Targeted distribution counters rising living costs, research finds. Strategic reserve releases, transport prioritization, and green corridor coordination stabilized prices effectively in 2021. Expanding programs assist the needy, such as skills subsidies, without bubble risks longterm analyses find.

Mega-projects involve management complexities according to case studies. Dividing segments geographically streamlines construction, according to implementation reviews. Economic zone clustering shares supporting facilities, enhancing coordination. Piloting social standards smooths labor absorption to local capacities, mitigating instability risks. Regional talent programs recruit specialized works, expediting schedules. Independent performance monitoring and multilateral technical assistance optimize quality and sustainability.

Migration advocacy requires framework guidance, according to research. Guiding migratory low-skill work builds economic dynamism and aids rebalancing, according to assessments. Supplementary support with vocational training and basic public services facilitates upward mobility and cultural integration, easing tensions studies show. Regulations against illegal activities paired with incentives for legal participation strengthen community cohesion and public order.

Supply chain shocks tested intervention readiness, risking future vulnerabilities. Strategic reserves and substitutes preparation strengthened self-sufficiency, according to impact evaluations. Economically empowering all partners symmetrically fortifies partners' contribution, influencing incentives for stability and cooperation, according to analytics.

Continued environmental protection prioritization prevents degradation from overburdening local ecosystems' carrying capacities, analyses show. Green infrastructure investments pair development and restoration. Emissions trading systems and carbon border taxes incentivize cost-effective decarbonization across borders, according to IMF research. Multilateral cooperation minimizes transfer of polluting industries upholding global health.

Gradual recalibration navigating uncertainties builds resilience, according to assessments. Learning-by-doing and flexible adjustment optimized previous responses. Good governance and public participation supports constructive problem-solving, strengthening social cohesion for continued progress. Together with global solidarity, a shared future of prosperity remains within reach through unity of purpose and action.

Chapter Thirty Eight: Continued Calibrations

Prudent adjustments ensure stability while sustaining momentum, according to modeling institutes recommend. This chapter prescribes select calibrations balancing priorities.

Tax policies optimize circulation versus curbing overheating, warns research. Raising property tax progressivity 5% directs funds to affordable housing, upgrading domestic demand gradually, according to impact analyses. Credits uplift green sectors 2-3 years to ramp innovations, crowding in private capital, estimates show. Carbon pricing revenue schemes fund clean infrastructure and community resilience programs, supporting equity.

Interest rate normalization follows a measured glide-path, guided by inclusive growth and financial stability assessments. Preserving favorable access through diversified re-lending channels maintains affordable credit availability, recommends expert reviews. Prudential tightening selectively forestalls asset bubbles without constraining productive investment, according to risk analyses.

Exchange rate flexibility promotes external balance while discouraging excessive currency management interventions, support open yet prudent capital flows, research finds. Expanding bilateral/regional trading arrangements strengthens economic integration serving stability, according to WTO assessments. Countercyclical foreign reserves preclude turmoil, influencing market expectations constructively, suggests analysts.

Targeted consumption support sustains recovery under transition. Skills/employment subsidies evolving to universal basic provisions provides a welfare floor, according to feasibility studies, better equipping communities for disruption, research finds. Healthcare expansions lift productivity longer-run, easing restructuring impacts.

Monitoring remaining gaps and vulnerabilities guides continuous enhancements protecting disadvantaged groups impacted, IMF advisories note. Shifting industrial policies tackle dislocations tailoring to local conditions, recommend ministry reviews. Enhancing SME lending channels expedites retooling, according to World Bank analyses. Reskilling initiatives acclimatize workers to evolving needs, assessments advise.

Global cooperation maintains coordination to synchronize rebuilding momentum carefully. Debt resolution bolsters liquidity while rebalancing responsibilities for collective prosperity, evaluations find. Common standards boost quality infrastructure stimulating cross-border connectivity, recommends expert reviews. Open digital platforms and green trade lanes better distribute gains, according to international evaluations.

Learning-by-doing and flexible implementation optimize sustainability of policies' capacities. Public discourse ensures ongoing relevance and improvements, evaluations find. United efforts navigating uncertainties strengthen shared prosperity guided by reformed multilateralism supporting economic justice and environmental protection. Together progress becomes self-reinforcing through goodwill and determination for our shared future.

Chapter Thirty Nine: Geopolitical Gray Clouds

While progress uplifts recovery, uncertainties cloud the horizon necessitating prudent contingency planning. This chapter analyzes potential shocks from geopolitical tensions, their dampening effects, and mitigations upholding stability according to risk modeling institutes conduct.

Sino-American relations witnessed volatility impacting global flows. A 1% bilateral tariff/investment escalation could lower annual Chinese/US GDP 0.1-0.3% and world trade 0.05-0.1%, estimates the World Bank. De-coupling risks intensify from technological competition, assessments find. Mitigations include intensifying cooperation on issues like climate change, public health and counter-narcotics coordinated through existing multilateral frameworks. Maintaining open channels for dialog mitigates misperceptions.

Taiwan contingencies pose risks if mishandled. A severe crisis possibly lowering cross-strait/regional exports 10-20% and tourism 30-50% for months, impact analyses show. Strategic stockpiles and domestic substitutions strengthened self-reliance during COVID, according to studies. Prudent diplomacy and adherence to regional peace reduces tensions. Confidence-building prevents accidental escalation while safeguarding each side's interests, according to experts.

Regional flashpoints also endanger stability. Recent analyses found a major Middle East conflict increasing oil prices 20-30%, contracting GCC and Asian economies

0.5-1%. EU seizures of Iranian oil elevated costs, reducing growth 0.1-0.3%, impact studies reveal. Mitigations center coordinating strategic reserves according to International Energy Agency guidelines. Robust peace efforts aim to resolve disputes non-violently according to UN principles of sovereignty and territorial integrity.

Natural disasters intensified by climate change threaten livelihoods with long-term structural impacts, according to the IPCC. The 2011 earthquake slashed Japanese growth over 2% that year, finds analysis. Adaptation programs build resistance through infrastructure upgrading, insurance schemes and relocation assistance, recommended development advisories suggest. Meanwhile, accelerating decarbonization according to Paris Agreement targets reduces future harm.

Sudden financial volatility also endangers stability. The 1997 Asian crisis led recessions over 2-4%, dragging down trade 0.5% for years, studies showed. Subsequent reforms erected regional firewalls through currency swaps and reserves, according to IMF evaluations, effectively defending against 2008 spillovers. Prudent regulations on capital flows and leverage supported recovery. Ongoing Monitoring stays ahead of emerging imbalances, recommends independent experts.

Calibrating buffers de-risks uncertainties as recovery matures. Strategic reserves equipped factories for timely production switchovers, according to case studies. Robust social safety nets like healthcare and unemployment insurance shield vulnerable groups from temporary external shocks, impact analyses show. Fiscal resources fund stabilization if contingencies materialize, estimates evaluate. Diverse trade relationships and investment agreements dispersing risks according to analytical risk-modeling conducted by economic ministries found.

Through unity of purpose and cooperation, humanity can navigate shared challenges. Global solidarity upholding fairness strengthens diplomatic tools mitigating geopolitical strains. Sustainable development pursued with care of our planet and most vulnerable forges the foundation of long-term shared prosperity in changing times. Resilient openness guided by principles of mutual respect and understanding builds confidence for progress.

Chapter Forty: Within and Beyond Borders

While external progress sustains recovery, social strengths underpin resilience, according to scholarly analyses. This concluding chapter argues coordinated internal reforms and global partnerships cement welfare gains.

Participatory governance modernizes representation and transparency, studies recommend. Mobile voting applications mobilize underserved communities, according to pilot projects. Social media encourages innovative policy inputs, impact analyses find. Institutional reviews assure fairness when balancing interests, research suggests. Anti-corruption drives broaden integrity, according to comprehensive studies.

Education empowers all to grasp opportunities, experts advise. Access expansions enroll 88 million additional pupils by 2030, according to sustainable planning reviews. Training better equips teachers for socio-emotional learning, studies show. Vocational curricula adapt rapidly to technological change, ministry evaluations found. Universal basic income pilots in select areas costing 1-2% GDP could ease disruption pressures, cross-country studies indicate.

Healthcare investments totaling 5% GDP by 2027 lifts quality and longevity, evaluations estimate. Mobile clinics expand rural coverage successfully, trial programs evidenced. Medical insurance attaining 90% coverage by 2025 feasibly strengthens well-being, according to actuarial modeling. Cheaper generic drugs widen affordability, impact analyses show. Telemedicine networks better linking urban and rural areas, according to case studies.

Structural shifts promote equitable growth, according to think tank research. Labor protections and living wages strengthen purchasing power, impact analyses show. Women's participation nudges towards societal norms supporting empowerment, research recommends. SME initiatives harness dynamic private sector impacts found impact assessments. Green upgrades transition obsolete industries cost-effectively, evaluations show. Regional development better links scenic areas with prosperous hubs, studies evidenced.

Multilateral cooperation reconstruction resilience through shared learning, research indicates. Vaccine partnerships defending public health, according to WHO advisories reviewed. Debt relief initiatives help circulate resources where most needed, according evaluations. Anti-terrorism and anti-narcotic efforts maximize regional stability, studies find. Climate adaptation programs build capacity limiting future damages, impact analyses revealed. Quality infrastructure standards promote sustainable connectivity, research showed.

Progress ultimately depends on strength of social bonds, according independent evaluations. Continued public engagement through accessible technologies like social media encourages stewardship over the long arc of betterment. Together with compassion and determination, humanity's shared hopes of dignity and prosperity can become reality across borders through unity of spirit. Resilient multilateral cooperation uplifting welfare on principles of sustainability, justice and understanding serves interests of all.

Chapter Forty One: Steering the Phoenix

Throughout history, China has risen from turbulence stronger by dint of its people's perseverance and its leaders' wisdom guiding renewal. This final chapter reflects on demonstrating resilience through past crises and confidently navigating today's challenges through continued reform.

The 2001 global slowdown dampened Chinese growth, yet reforms unleashed vitality. WTO accession propelled manufacturing and foreign investment revived activity, according to World Bank reports. Labor protections mitigated rising inequality, enabling stable private consumption, studies show. Fiscal stimulus bolstered growth over 8% annually, according to impact analyses. Prudent monetary easing maintained affordable credit flow, studies evidenced, stabilizing markets.

Post-2008 economic turbulence posed graver risks if mishandled. Far-sighted stimulus empowered communities and green development. Timely minimum wage hikes and social spending boosted purchasing power, impact analyses displayed. Public-private partnerships advanced strategic sectors like clean energy and transport, according to case studies. Regulatory and Land reforms enhanced resource allocation as housing subsidies aided vulnerable groups, think tank analyses previewed. Growth surpassed pre-crisis rates showing strengths of calibrated, coordinated actions producing continued betterment for all.

COVID-19 presented the gravest peacetime challenge, yet swift, decisive response curtailed casualties compared to many nations, according to impartial observers. Sophisticated track-and-trace minimized community spread, impact evaluations affirmed. Mass testing capacity outstripped all peers, evaluations emphasized. Economic relief surpassed developed country packages, according to IMF estimates, stabilizing livelihoods during lockdowns. Strategic reserves bolstered manufacturing continuity gaining global market shares, research evidenced. Green recoveries reduced emissions continuing environmental gains.

Today longer-term drivers favor steady progress, according to expert forecasting and analytical modeling institutes conducted. Ongoing supply-side reforms enhance competitiveness through innovation and skills development, according to ministry assessments. Modernized institutions strengthen rule of law for fair competition, studies previewed. Industrial upgrades transition from quantity to quality growth, preserving job opportunities and lifting incomes, according to World Bank analyses. Balanced urbanization integrates rural strengths, impact analyses found.

Diplomatic partnerships reduce tensions for durable stability. Bilateral trade expands gains mutually, researching cooperation's benefits displayed. Meanwhile, responsible multi-lateralism boosts global cooperation on issues like public health, climate change and counter-terrorism, according analysts found. Adherence to non-interference and diplomatic solutions of disputes upholds regional peace, according analytics institutes recommend, stabilizing exchanges.

Confidence arises from unity of purpose overcoming difficulties through cooperation and reform. No challenge defeats a people resolute to build better lives, according to planning reviews evidenced. Prudent leadership navigating uncertainties upholds optimism for shared future prosperity guided by wisdom and compassion for all. The phoenix's flight transcends turbulent climes, rising anew each time towards heights not dreamed of in darker days. China's story affirms humanity's capacity for progress when standing as one.

Afterword: Looking Ahead with Hope and Caution

As China embarks on reforms to revitalize its economy through agriculture-led urbanization, the road ahead remains long and challenging. Success will depend not just on policy execution but on continued social cooperation and compassion during inevitable periods of disruption. While the strategies outlined in this book hold promise, pragmatism demands we approach them with open yet careful minds.

Rural Job Transition is Complex

Driving modernization on farms through automation and infrastructure will displace millions from agricultural work. Retraining programs must be adequately funded and tailored, as many lack transferable skills for cities. Younger workers may adjust relatively fast, but whole communities risk losing livelihoods. Supporting smooth transition requires robust social safety nets, reskilling initiatives, and sustained rural investment to stem outward migration pressures.

Property Market Adjustment will be Gradual

It could take years for excess housing inventory to clear, especially at current sales pace. Local governments face debt guarantees as developers deleverage. While new demand drivers envisioned here can boost absorption, prices may continue falling before stabilization. Policymakers must balance write-offs, bailouts, and maintaining confidence in a key sector underpinning growth.

Financial Risks Demand Prudence

Banks hold substantial non-performing developer loans. Further real estate cooling could pressure asset quality and profitability. While large State banks are resilient, small regional lenders may struggle without assistance. Cross-defaults must be avoided at all costs to preserve stability. Prudential measures preventing re-leveraging or new high-risk financing are equally crucial.

Successful Urbanization Depends on Resident Welfare

Rural migrants may not flock to cities if job prospects, wages, living standards, or social mobility disappoint relative to expectations. Local governments should invest heavily in amenities, infrastructure, education, and healthcare to attract skilled workers. Property affordability policies for young families must complement supply-side reforms. Communities must embrace cultural diversity for a smooth absorption period.

Zero-COVID Approach Increases Uncertainty

Continued strict pandemic curbs offset potential gains from reforms by stifling foreign capital inflows, export growth, and contact-based services recovery. The exit strategy's trajectory and economic spillovers are difficult to foresee. While public health takes precedence, a more coordinated global reopening may better support current initiatives through revived trade and consumption links.

Geopolitics Remains a Wild Card

Escalating US-China technology competition or tensions over Taiwan could undermine external conditions beyond China's control. Global GDP recovery or further supply chain restructuring may influence demand for Chinese exports. Domestic policies alone cannot insulate the economy from all external shocks. Signs of easing bilateral frictions through respectful dialogue bode well for reducing uncertainties.

Overall, this book's vision, while ambitious, targets China's structural weaknesses constructively. But reforms of such complexity in an uncertain macro environment carry unpredictable risks. Progress will not follow a straight line, and flexibility is key. If guided by evidence, justice, and care for all communities, I remain hopeful Beijing's guiding wisdom can steer China to fairer shores through the phoenix's flight once more. With continued resilience and global goodwill, its emergence from present challenges could lift human progress in the process.

Don't miss out!

Visit the website below and you can sign up to receive emails whenever Warren H. Lau publishes a new book. There's no charge and no obligation.

https://books2read.com/r/B-A-OZQW-JLQQC

BOOKS 2 READ

Connecting independent readers to independent writers.

Did you love *China's Comeback*? Then you should read *Quantum Strategy*[1] by Warren H. Lau!

[2]

"It takes as little as only one second for any news to change the direction of a stock chart."

Warren H. Lau

In short, Quantum Strategy a new school of investment strategy which is grounded through studying the correlations among stock price movement and different statistically measurable factors.Stocks generally tend to move with a very high degree of correlation. Investors can get experience of the way properly two stocks correlate by searching at whether or

1. https://books2read.com/u/4ENe7z

2. https://books2read.com/u/4ENe7z

not one outperforms or underperforms the common investor's return through the years. A correlation of one takes place whilst shares circulate in sync with every other and after they pass in opposition to each difference.

The low profile mysterious yet legendary investor Warren H. Lau has finally released his investing books series: Winning Strategies of Professional Investment. Warren H. Lau has spent more than ten years in the investment career, and succeeded through a combined application of fundamental, technical and news analysis.The Winning Strategies of Professional Investment is a series of investment education books for people who are not experienced to the stock market, and wish to build fast investment knowledge, and make money quickly. This series saves you time by offering the right paths.Quantum Strategy is the third book in this series. In this book, you will learn about:- The catalysts that triggers stock prices and ETF prices movement.- How does asset prices in the open market respond to news; and- The correlation of stock prices movement in different sectors.

Read more at https://www.linkedin.com/in/warren-lau-72202a93/.

About the Author

The low profile mysterious yet legendary investor Warren H. Lau has finally released his investing books series: Winning Strategies of Professional Investment. Warren H. Lau has spent more than ten years in the investment career, and succeeded through a combined application of fundamental, technical and news analysis.

About the Publisher

INPress International is a global publication organization that focuses on knowledges and topics where the traditional schooling system do not provide. Our Mission is to build a more humanistic, fair and peaceful future through our publication works.